THE ROMAN EMPIRE THE EMPIRE OF THE EDOMITE.

BY

WILLIAM BEESTON,

OF THE HONOURABLE SOCIETY OF LINCOLN'S INN, AND SOMETIME OF QUEENS COLLEGE, CAMBRIDGE.

LONDON:

(FOR THE AUTHOR).

GEORGE COX, 18 KING STREET, COVENT GARDEN.

1853.

"IF THE WHOLE SCHEME OF SCRIP-
"TURE EVER COMES TO BE UNDERSTOOD,
"BEFORE THE RESTITUTION OF ALL
"THINGS, AND WITHOUT MIRACULOUS
"INTERPOSITIONS, IT MUST BE IN THE
"SAME WAY AS NATURAL KNOWLEDGE
"IS COME AT: BY THE CONTINUANCE
"AND PROGRESS OF LEARNING AND
"LIBERTY; AND BY PARTICULAR PER-
"SONS ATTENDING TO, COMPARING,
"AND PURSUING, INTIMATIONS SCAT-
"TERED UP AND DOWN, WHICH ARE
"OVERLOOKED AND DISREGARDED BY
"THE GENERALITY OF THE WORLD."—
BISHOP BUTLER'S ANALOGY OF RELIGION TO THE CONSTITUTION AND COURSE OF NATURE.

THE ROMAN EMPIRE, &c.

In the first year of the reign of Belshazzar king of Babylon, the prophet DANIEL had a dream, and visions of his head upon his bed. "I saw," writes the prophet,* "in my vision by night, and behold the four winds of heaven strove upon the great sea, and FOUR BEASTS came up from the sea, diverse one from another. THE FIRST was like a LION, and had eagle's wings. And behold, another beast, A SECOND, like to a BEAR; and it raised itself up on one side; and it had three ribs in the mouth of it, between the teeth of it. After this, I beheld, and lo ANOTHER, like a LEOPARD, which had upon the back of it FOUR WINGS OF A FOWL; this beast had also FOUR HEADS. After this, I

* Dan. vii.

saw in the night visions, and behold a FOURTH BEAST, dreadful and terrible, and strong exceedingly; and it had great iron teeth: it devoured, and brake in pieces, and stamped the residue with the feet of it: and it was DIVERSE FROM ALL THE BEASTS THAT WERE BEFORE IT; and it had TEN HORNS. I saw in the night visions, and behold, ONE LIKE THE SONS OF MEN came with the clouds of heaven, and came to the ANCIENT OF DAYS, and they brought HIM near before HIM. And there was given HIM dominion, and glory, and a kingdom; that all peoples, nations, and languages should serve HIM * * * * I came near unto one of them that stood by, and asked him the truth of all this. So he told me, and made me know the interpretation of the things. These great beasts, which are four, are FOUR KINGS which must arise OUT OF THE EARTH. The fourth beast will be the FOURTH KINGDOM UPON EARTH; which will be DIVERSE FROM ALL KINGDOMS, and will devour the whole earth, and will tread it down, and break it in pieces. But the judgment will sit, and his dominion will be taken away; and the kingdom, and dominion, and the greatness of the kingdom under the whole heaven, will be given to the PEOPLE OF THE SAINTS OF THE MOST HIGH; whose kingdom is an everlasting kingdom, and all dominions must serve and obey HIM."

The THREE FIRST BEASTS, or the empires of THE BABYLONIANS, THE PERSIANS, and THE MACEDONIANS, having successively passed away, the FOURTH BEAST, or KINGDOM, of the prophecy stood revealed in the iron domination of THE ROMANS; and to the consequent enquiry, WHENCE CAME THE ROMANS? that people have insisted on replying, in the words of their great poet, "AB ORIS TROJÆ: GENUS UNDE LATINUM; ALBANIQUE PATRES; ATQUE ALTÆ MŒNIA ROMÆ."

ÆNEAS,* escaping from the destruction of Troy, after many adventures and dangers, arrived in Italy, where he was kindly received by LATINUS, the king of THE LATINS, who gave him his daughter in marriage. ÆNEAS built a city, which was called LAVINIUM, in honour of his wife. ASCANIUS, his son, succeeded to the kingdom, and to him SILVIUS, a second son; and the succession continued for more than three hundred years in the

* Goldsmith's Roman History.

family; NUMITOR, the fifteenth from Æneas, being the last king. ROMULUS and REMUS, the grandsons of Numitor, resolved to build a town upon the hills where they had lived as shepherds; and, REMUS being slain, ROMULUS laid the foundations of that city which was one day to give law to the world. It was called ROME."

* * * *

But this tradition, which commanded the implicit belief of the Romans themselves, and was held by them in almost religious reverence, has by the learned of our own times been rejected and discarded; and the story of a Trojan colony in Latium is now denounced as fabulous, poetical, and DESTITUTE* OF THE SLIGHTEST FOUNDATION IN HISTORICAL TRUTH. Still, the critical acumen which has been found powerful to destroy, has proved impotent to construct; it has deprived us of the ancient faith, but it does not offer us a better creed: at the present hour, all is confusion and conjecture; and the story of the foundation of Rome, and the people from whom THE ETERNAL CITY sprung, are admitted to be the very points about which the learned are most ignorant.†

* Niebuhr. † Ibid.

Unspeakable, then, must our astonishment be, when we perceive, that this grand secret was certainly discovered, and disclosed, more than twelve hundred years ago; that the true answer to the question WHENCE CAME THE ROMANS? may have been returned, and even registered in writing, before the birth of Christ; that the response proceeded neither from Greek nor Roman, but from the DESPISED JEW; that it has been preserved to us in the JEWISH TARGUMS; that it exists amidst the fables and impieties, the absurdities and the blasphemies, of the JEWISH TALMUD; and that it may be comprehended in these twenty words: THE ROMANS CAME FROM ESAU, WHO IS EDOM; AND ITALY IS THE IDUMEA, ROME THE BOZRAH, OF THE HEBREW PROPHETS.

* * * *

"The descendants of Esau," say the JEWISH RABBINS,* "the sworn enemies of the descendants of Jacob, even to the end of the world, were at first a small nation, inhabiting Mount Seir and the adjacent country, contiguous to the land of Canaan. They were easily confined within their own limits,

* Allen's Modern Judaism; London, 1816.

so long as the Israelites enjoyed a great and formidable empire in Canaan: but, after that the powerful republic of the twelve tribes had been destroyed by the Assyrians and Babylonians, they wonderfully increased in numbers and in strength; extended their dominion in the West; subjugated Italy; founded Rome, and the Roman Empire; and at length entirely overturned the Jewish state, the Second Temple being destroyed by Titus Vespasian; and, professing the religion of Jesus Christ, which they were the first of all nations to embrace, they hold Jacob in captivity till MESSIAH BEN DAVID shall appear." The Rabbins further assert, that the prophecies of the prophets against Esau, Edom, and the cities of Edom, have as yet received but a partial accomplishment; and that they will obtain their fulfilment in the punishment and destruction of ROME CHRISTIAN: they designate the Eternal City IMPIOUS ROME; they denominate her empire the IMPIOUS KINGDOM, or KINGDOM OF IMPIETY; and they believe, that the SON OF DAVID will not come until this IMPIOUS KINGDOM SHALL HAVE BEEN EXTENDED OVER THE WHOLE WORLD.

Such is the TRADITION OF THE RABBINS;

and PAPAL ROME has done her utmost to suppress it: but without success. The two citations following will be sufficient for our present purpose.

In the fourth chapter of the Lamentations of Jeremiah, it is written: "He will visit thine iniquity, O daughter of Edom." The Elder Buxtorf* extracts the paraphrase of this passage given by the Targumist, and translates the Chaldee of the original into Latin, by these words: "Isto tempore visitabo iniquitatem tuam, ROMAM IMPIAM, quæ ædificata es in Italia, et repleta es turbis hominum EX POSTERIS EDOM." And he adds, "Sic editiones duæ primæ Venetæ. In posterioribus, ROMA IMPIA, et sequentia verba, omissa sunt, declinandæ invidiæ causa, relicto spatio exiguo, cui Judæi manu inscribere solent omissa, ut factum in exemplari quod apud me est, et a Judæo care emptum." I have referred to a copy of the first edition of the Biblia Hebraica Rabbinnica, printed by Bomberg at Venice in the years 1517–8 and now in the Bodleian Library at Oxford, and find that it contains the passage as cited and translated by Buxtorf. There is, therefore, every reason to suppose that the reading of the first edition of the Bomberg Bible is the genuine paraphrase of the

* Lex. Chald. Talm. et Rabb. fol. 2228.

Targumist; and that the author of the Targum from which it is extracted was the true JONATHAN BEN UZZIEL. He is said by the Jews to have been a disciple of the famous Hillel; and to have flourished about one hundred years before the destruction of Jerusalem by the Romans.*

"Volumina Talmudica," writes Schoetgenius, "jussu Pontificis Maximi expurgata esse, res in vulgus est notissima. Quia vero editiones antiquæ non expurgatæ, Venetæ et Lublinensis, sunt rarissimæ, in gratia eorum qui editiones castratas possident. singula quæ expuncta sunt hic exponam." He then goes on to restore the original readings of various passages of the Talmud which have been thus mutilated, and amongst them he notices the twenty-third verse of the seventh chapter of Daniel; where it is said, that the Fourth Beast "shall devour the whole earth, and shall tread it down, and break it in pieces." He here introduces the commentary of Rabbi Jochanan. "Et comedet omnem terram, conculcabit et comminuat eam. Dixit Rabbi Jochanan, זו רומי חייבת: Intelligitur ROMA PECCATRIX." He adds, "Editione expurgata, loco רומי, Roma, habent

* Talmud. Cod. Shabbath, cap. i.

† Horæ Heb. et Talmud. tom. ii. 840.

פרם., Persam:" and he goes on to say, "Si vota hic quicquam valerent, ut illud exemplum Talmudis oculis usurpare potuerim, de quo sequentia narrat Michael de la Roche, tomo XIV Memoriarum Britannicarum. Il y a dans le bibliothèque publique d'Oxford, un exemplaire du Talmud de Babylon, imprimé à Venise en dix volumes en folio, lequel appartenoit à Selden. Cet exemplaire avoit été revu, conformement aux ordres de l' Inquisition, par un Capucin, qui a raturé tous les passages touchant le Messie, la Vierge Marie, les Apôtres, et les Evangelistes, et TOUS LES ENDROITS OÙ IL EST PARLÉ DE L'EMPIRE ROMAIN, que le Talmud appelle Malcuth Harasha'a, REGNUM IMPIUM. Ces passages raturés ne sont point lisibles; l'encre a tellement penetré le papier, que l'on ne sauroit même lire les mots de la page opposée." — The Jochanan here mentioned is the famous Rabbin Jochanan Ben Zaccai, of whom it was said, that the glory of wisdom ceased when Jochanan died. His constitutions and sayings are frequently referred to in the Mishna,* which must have been completed, at the latest, by the year of our Lord 189. He was greatly favoured by Titus

* Cod. Succa, cap. iii. 12; cap. ii. 5. Cod. Ketuboth, cap. xiii. 1.

Vespasian; and died about two years after the destruction of Jerusalem by the Romans. He is said to have received the traditions from the mouth of Hillel himself.

* * * *

I propose, in the ensuing pages, to establish the certainty of this RABBINICAL TRADITION, and demonstrate the true ORIGIN OF THE ROMAN PEOPLE: first, by the testimony of LINGUAL ANALYSIS; and, secondly, by the evidence of the SURE WORD OF PROPHECY.

* * * *

Rome's builder was a LATIN; the first inhabitants of the city were Latins also, and it was, first as the head and leader, and afterwards as the mistress and sovereign of the CONFEDERATED LATINS, that Rome obtained the empire of the world. Rome's language, too, in all its stages, and in all its changes, was ever called the LATIN TONGUE; a certain proof that her original was neither Oscan, Tuscan, Umbrian, or anything but Latin. Yet, Rome was no colony of Alba, or of any other Latin town. Romulus, gathering together the Latin shepherds inhabiting the 'vastæ solitudines'* adjacent to the Tiber, built a

* Liv. lib. i. c. iv.

wall round them; and forthwith Rome was. The new-born city received into her veins a large infusion of Sabine blood: but this was more than compensated, and the Sabine element in her first population over-powered, by the destruction of Alba, and the subjugation of the other Latin States; after which, Rome and Latium were the selfsame thing. The notion of a Tuscan population, mixed with the Latin and the Sabine citizens of Romulus, is a dream. The first Tarquin was, no doubt, a Tuscan: but he entered Rome as a private citizen, disgusted with Tarquinii; and, to obtain Rome's franchise, had to change his name. Neither did the city rise slowly, and from insignificance; or climb by short and painful steps to a place amongst the Latins. The birth and rise of Rome were instantaneous. Like the fabled crop of Cadmus, she sprang from the earth armed to the teeth,* and ready, if not eager, for the fight; and from the first hour of her existence, she lived, and moved, and had her being, in total independence of the neighbour towns, and in avowed rivalry with them all. Whilst, therefore, we designate the Fourth Beast of Daniel's prophecy by the Hebrew words ממשל הרומה, MIMSHAL HAROMAH, TO IMPE-

* Liv. lib. i. c. 19.

RIUM ROMANUM; the Greek 'Η ΒΑΣΙΛΕΙΑ ΛΑΤΙΝΗ* will be equally descriptive of Rome's iron rule.

The Romans, then, being Latins, the Latins themselves must, according to our RABBINICAL TRADITION, be Idumeans; and our first business, therefore, lies with the origin, history, and language of the ancient Edomites. To the consideration of these questions I now go on; observing, in passing, that, using their component letters as numerals, each of these names, MIMSHAL HAROMAH, and HE LATINE BASILEIA, contains the number SIX HUNDRED AND SIXTY-SIX; the NUMBER OF THE NAME of the APOCALYPTIC BEAST, "Here is wisdom," writes St. John: "let him that hath understanding count THE NUMBER (of the name) OF THE BEAST; for it is the NUMBER (of the name) OF A MAN; and his number (the number of his name), is SIX HUNDRED THREESCORE AND SIX."

* * * * *

Forty years old was ISAAC, when he took to wife REBEKAH, the daughter of Bethuel the Syrian; and, at the age of nearly sixty years, the

* Adam Clarke, Comm. on Rev.

patriarch intreated the Almighty for his wife, because she was barren. And Isaac's prayer was heard and answered: Rebekah conceived; and the children STRUGGLED TOGETHER within her. The circumstance was, evidently, preternatural, and of repeated occurrence; for Rebekah went to inquire of the Lord, and said, "Why am I thus?" The Divine response was given in the words following. "TWO NATIONS ARE IN THY WOMB, AND TWO MANNER OF PEOPLE WILL BE SEPARATED FROM THY BOWELS; AND THE ONE PEOPLE WILL BE STRONGER THAN THE OTHER PEOPLE; AND THE ELDER WILL SERVE THE YOUNGER." These are the infant struggles of two contending nations, descendants of twin brothers, to whom thou wilt give birth: of these peoples, the one will be greatly stronger than the other; and the descendants of the elder will be made the servants of the younger, brother.

Rebekah's days to be delivered were fulfilled; and, behold, there were twins in her womb. The first came forth all hairy, covered with hair as with a hairy garment; and the HAIR WAS RED. They called him ESAU. The other, in the birth, catches his elder brother by the heel; and, from that circumstance, is named JACOB, HE-WILL-TRIP-UP-(MEN'S)-HEELS. The appellation ESAU has never, I believe, been interpreted. I take it to be Syriac; and to be compounded of עֶשׂ, ES (Hebrew אֵשׁ, ESH), FIRE, FLAME, the definite O, and HU, (HE IS). These words being brought together, the Zekofo, or O, will change to Pethoco, A; the HE, or H, will be expelled from the text; and the vowels A and U will form a diphthong:* thus: ESOHU, ESAHU, ESAU: A-FIREBRAND-IS-HE. I have not been able to discover the word, in the simple form, in the Syriac; but there are, I think, clear traces of its existence in the earlier periods of that language. Thus Schindler,† speaking of the Hebrew אָשַׁשׁ, ASHASH, says, "Respexit ad אֵשׁ, ESH;" and, accordingly, we find the Syriac‡ verb אַשֵּׁשׁ, ASES, INFLAMMAVIT. The name would, therefore, appear to have been suggested, not merely by the hairiness of Esau, but by the colour of his hair; and we learn from it that this colour was fiery red, SCARLET. We

* Phillips's Syriac Grammar, London, 1837, p. 10.

† Lex. Pentaglott. fol. 1653.

‡ Castell. Lex. Syr. cur. I. D. Michaelis, Goett. 1788, page 661. Ibid. ܐܫܫܘܬܐ ܕܥܠܡܐ Conflagratio mundi.

seem to be here put into possession of a circumstance of domestic history: the Hebrew father names one son, and the Syrian mother the other; and each child derives his appellation from the naming parent's mother-tongue.

The boys grew: Esau became a cunning hunter, a man of the field; but Jacob was a plain man, dwelling in tents. Esau was the favourite of Isaac, and this, because the patriarch did eat of his venison; but Rebekah's favourite was Jacob. Amongst other accomplishments of a life which, compared with Esau's, was sedentary and civilized, Jacob possessed skill in cookery; he sod (was in the habit, that is, of sodding,) a certain red pottage, of which Esau seems to have been particularly fond, and the composition of which Jacob, it appears, kept to himself. The partiality of Esau for this food proved the turning point in the fortunes of the predicted nations. "And Jacob sod pottage. And Esau came from the field; and he was faint. And he said to Jacob, Feed me, I pray thee, with that same red pottage; for I am faint. And Jacob said, Sell me this day thy birthright. And Esau said, Behold I am at the point to die: and WHAT PROFIT shall this birthright do to ME? And Jacob said, Swear to me this day: and he sware unto him; and sold his birthright to Jacob." "Thus," writes Moses, "did Esau despise his birthright;" and St. Paul declares that, so doing, he became a 'profane man.'

Now, this transaction appears to be grievously misunderstood; and the conduct of Jacob towards his brother most unjustly condemned. The birthright sold by Esau was the possession (not by himself, but his descendants) of two third-parts of the promised land; this gift of God to Abraham being divisible amongst all the sons of Isaac (in whom alone the patriarch's seed was called) in such manner as that the eldest son should have the 'double portion.' It is extraordinary that, with the express testimony of Scripture to the contrary, the commentators should insist that Esau's birthright included the future priesthood, and the glory of becoming the progenitor of the Christ of God. "Reuben, (writes the author of First Chronicles,*) was the firstborn of Israel; but, forasmuch as he defiled his father's bed, his birthright was given unto the sons of Joseph. But the genealogy (of the chief ruler) is not to be reckoned after (has no connection with) the birthright: for (as to this) Judah prevailed

* 1 Chron. v. 1.

above his brethren; and of him (comes, not came) the chief ruler;" (the Nagid, or Prince; the Messiah; called by Daniel* Mashiakh Nagid, Messiah the Prince). The birthright, or second portion of Reuben, was given to the sons of Joseph; and Ephraim and Manasseh inherited in Canaan as two of the tribes of Israel: but the priesthood fell to Levi; and, "It is evident," writes the author of Hebrews, "that our Lord sprang out of Judah." The charge made against Jacob is, then, that seeing his brother about to perish of hunger, he took advantage of his distress, and purchased (not for himself, but for his descendants) the right to inherit all the promised land. The notion is utterly incredible, and is in direct contradiction of the sacred text. Esau is dwelling in the tents of Isaac and Rebekah; the tents of a mighty prince;† supplied with all the necessaries and all the elegancies of the nomade life. He returns from a common hunting excursion; faint indeed, but not dying of hunger: he asks not for food in general, and to sustain life, but he requires to be fed with a special delicacy; 'Feed me, I pray thee, with that same red pottage.' He does not part with his expectancies to

* Dan. ix. 25.

† Gen. xxvi. 12, 13, 14, 16.

preserve existence; but he basely sells the glorious heritage of his children for 'one morsel of meat,' a single mess of this red pottage. 'Skin after skin, yea, all that a man hath will he give for his life:' and, had Esau done no more, the Apostle had never charged him with profaneness. The words 'Behold, I am at the point to die,' refer to the reversionary character of the promised heritage. More than three hundred years had yet to pass, before the seed of Isaac would become entitled to the actual possession of Canaan; and therefore the gift was worth nothing to Esau himself; it will do no more good to ME, says he, than it would, if at this very moment I were about to die. Wherefore, he rejects God's grace; and, caring nothing for his descendants, sells their inheritance for one meal of pottage. The Apostle's charge against him is, that for a morsel of food, which he might well have gone without, he sold his birthright, and despised the gift of God; and Saint Paul draws from the conduct of this eldest son of Isaac a most impressive warning. Be ye not like unto Esau. For each of you, says the Apostle, addressing the Hebrew converts, there is reserved a birthright, a portion in the heavenly Canaan; granted to you by God as of His free gift, through Christ.

If, now, you should go backward, and, for the sake of the gratifications and enjoyments of this life, which are present and momentary, forfeit your claim to the heritage reserved for you in heaven, which is reversionary and afar off, you play the part of Esau; you sell your birthright for a mess of pottage; you become 'profane men.' The temptation, in all probability, originated with Esau himself; and was ordained by the Almighty to prove the man: to show what was in his heart; to cause him to testify against himself that he had no respect to the Divine promises; that he set no value on the gift of God. We may suppose him to have said, What would I not give for a taste of that red pottage! to eat of it I would part with the half of all that I am worth. And Jacob buys the birthright for a trifle: yet h gives the price set upon it by the elder brother. And, doubtless, Jacob's aim was self-protection, and regard for the interests of the chosen seed. For, as Esau had the power of alienating this heritage, he might have sold it to the sons of any other people; and so have made the Moabites, or the Philistines, co-heritors with the seed of Abraham: and Israel, suffering what the Almighty had put it in his power to prevent, would have proved himself as 'profane' a man as was his brother Esau.

The blessing which Esau would afterwards have inherited, and which he then sought with tears, was inseparably annexed to the promised land; and, in consenting to receive it from his father Isaac, Esau was the aggressor, and endeavoured to deprive Jacob of his undoubted right. If we compare the words of this blessing with the terms of that afterwards bestowed on Esau, we prove the fact at once. The DWELLING mentioned in the last, has no place in the former; and this, because the dwelling-place of the chosen seed had been already fixed: "Unto thee, even unto thy seed, will I give all these countries," were the words* of God to Isaac. It is evident, therefore, that the sale of Esau's birthright had been carefully concealed by him from his father; and that Isaac, blessing the elder son, intended to bless the younger also: for, as to one third of Canaan, the inheritance was ever Jacob's. God had given this land to the seed of Isaac: but the Almighty might have laid their heritage waste; or, granting it fertility, have caused it to become the basest of the kingdoms. The blessing which Isaac, by the Spirit

* Gen. xxvi. 3.

of prophecy, was enabled to pronounce, had reference solely to the character and political importance of the promised land, and not to its locality. "God will give thee of the dew of heaven, and of the fatness of the earth, and plenty of corn and wine; peoples will serve thee, and nations will bow down to thee; be thou the ruler of thy brethren, and thy mother's sons shall bow down to thee: cursed is he that curseth thee; and blessed is he that blesseth thee." Now, the mode in which Jacob obtained this blessing was prescribed to him by his mother Rebekah. "Upon me," said the wife of Isaac, "be thy curse:" in other words, no curse can follow compliance with my request. Isaac, indeed, 'trembled with an exceeding great trembling' (as well the patriarch might), when, for the first time, he learned that his beloved son had forfeited all title to the grace of God; and had, as it were, flung the gift of heaven in the great Giver's face: but, constrained by the Spirit which spake by him, he forthwith adds, "Yea, and he must be blessed." In this transaction, Isaac was the prophet of the Lord; and to impose upon the patriarch was, therefore, to lie to the Holy Ghost. The Queen of Israel made the attempt, and what was the result? "Come in, thou wife of

Jeroboam, why feignest thou thyself to be another?" were the sightless seer's words. And so with Jacob and Rebekah. We might expect to hear from Isaac, 'How is it that ye have agreed together to tempt the Spirit of the Lord? ye have not lied unto man, but unto God.' Yet, the imposition is not detected; the punishment of Ananias and Sapphira does not follow the attempt. Far otherwise: no sooner has the supposed crime been committed, than we hear the Almighty approving the deed, and blessing the chief actor in the fraud. "I am the Lord God of Abraham thy father, and the God of Isaac: the land whereon thou liest, to thee will I give it, and to thy seed: and, behold, I am with thee, and will keep thee in all places whither thou goest." Let God be true, and every man a liar: let us eschew, as manifestly false, all interpretations of Scripture which impugn the justice and the holiness of the Lord. The blessing was wholly Jacob's; the mode in which it was conferred was suggested by Rebekah: and she did what she did, to spare, as far as might be, the feelings, and mitigate the sufferings, of the aged, sightless, Isaac, consequent on the discovery of the degeneracy of his favourite son. But was not Jacob himself among the prophets? And

Isaac said, "Art thou my very son FIREBRAND? and Jacob said, I AM." "And the house of Jacob shall be a fire, and the house of Joseph a flame, and the house of Esau for stubble: for the Lord hath spoken it."* The answer of Jacob finds its parallels in the words of God to Abraham, "Take now thy son, thine ONLY SON, Isaac;" and in those passages † of the writings of Saint Paul, and of Josephus, where Isaac is denominated the patriarch's ONLY-BEGOTTEN SON. Ishmael and Esau being both cast out, Jacob became the only-begotten son of Abraham and Isaac, the sole inheritor of the promises of the Lord; and his title to the name 'Firebrand' was already registered in the decrees of God.

But the great and exceeding bitter cry of Esau, "Hast thou but one blessing, O my father? bless me, even me also," was both heard and answered by the Almighty: the Spirit of prophecy descended upon Isaac for the second time; and the destinies of the sons of Esau were revealed. "Behold, thy DWELLING shall be of the FATNESS OF THE EARTH, and of the DEW OF HEAVEN

* Obad. 18.

† Heb. xi. 17; Joseph. Antiq. lib. i. c. 13, 1.

from above; and by THY SWORD SHALT THOU LIVE; and thou shalt SERVE THY BROTHER; and it shall come to pass, CAASHÈR TARÌD, that thou shalt break his yoke from off thy neck." I quote a part of this prophecy in the original Hebrew; because the word TARÌD is susceptible of two widely-differing interpretations. First, with the Jewish commentators, we may derive this word from RADAH, DOMINARI: "And it shall come to pass that, when THOU SHALT HAVE THE DOMINION, thou shalt break his yoke from off thy neck." TARÌD may also be deduced from RUD, TO WANDER ABOUT, TO WANDER FAR AWAY: "And it shall come to pass that, WHEN THOU SHALT BECOME A WANDERER, thou shalt break his yoke from off thy neck." It is evident that there is nothing in the history of the Edomites, as hitherto understood, by which this portion of the prophecy can possibly have been accomplished: but, if the Æneas of the Roman story and his followers, if the whole Latin people, were Idumeans, then this great prophecy has been fulfilled in both the meanings put upon the word TARÌD. Now, we learn from Dionysius of Halicarnassus, that all did not admit that this Æneas was a Trojan. "Some historians," says Dionysius,* "affirm that Æneas (the Æneas of Homer) did not even come into Italy; and some, that he (the Æneas who did come) was another Æneas, not the son of Venus and Anchises."

The expectations of Rebekah were fulfilled: Esau's anger passed away; and we find him meeting Jacob, on the return of the latter from Padan-Aram, in perfect amity and peace. "And Esau ran to meet him, and embraced him, and fell upon his neck, and kissed him; and they wept." The reconciliation of the two brothers was complete. They afterwards buried their father Isaac in the sepulchre of Abraham, in the field of Machpelah, before Mamre; and thereupon Esau retired from Canaan, and "from the face of his brother Jacob, and dwelt in Seir: for their riches were more than that they might dwell together; the land wherein they were strangers could not bear them, because of their cattle."

On the approach of Esau, Jacob obtained from the Almighty the great name ISRAEL; an appellation which contains the prophetic history of the Jewish race. The patriarch at first supposed the intentions of his brother towards him to be hostile: and "he

* Antiq. Rom. lib. i. c. 53.

was greatly afraid and distressed; and he divided the people that was with him, and the flocks, and the herds, into two bands; and he said, If Esau come to the one company, and smite it, then the other company which is left may escape." "And Jacob was left alone; and there wrestled a man with him until the breaking of the day. And when he saw that he prevailed not against him, he touched the hollow of his thigh; and the hollow of Jacob's thigh was out of joint, as he wrestled with him. And he said, Let me go, for the day breaketh; and he said, I will not let thee go, except thou bless me." Then the DEITY discovers Himself. "And HE said unto him, What is thy name? and he said, JACOB," HEEL-TRIPPER; I have no better name. "And HE said, Thy name shall no more be called Jacob, but ISRAEL," (AS-)GOD-SHALL-HE-WRESTLE; "KI SARÌTHA IM ELOHÌM, VEÌM ANASHÌM VATTUCÀL:" "FOR WITH GOD HAST THOU WRESTLED, AND WITH MEN MUST THOU PREVAIL." He that has wrestled with God, without being thrown, must needs be victorious in all his wrestlings with mankind. The name is compounded of יִשְׂרֶה, ISRÈ, HE SHALL WRESTLE, and אֵל, EL, GOD; the Caph of similitude, or the word

'AS,' being understood, and the Segol (or E) of the verb changed into Kamets, (the long A,) as the sign of the proper-name, and in accordance with a rule hereafter to be stated. ISRE-EL, ISRAÈL, AS-GOD-SHALL-HE-WRESTLE. Both the patriarch's names are agonistic terms; and each of them is the opposite of the other. JACOB is the wrestler who, inferior to his adversary in strength, makes up for the deficiency by his adroitness; and so 'supplants,' that is, 'trips up,' his opponent: ISRAEL is the wrestler who at once lifts his antagonist off his legs, and hurls him backward to the earth. Do we seek a Scripture commentary on this great name? We have it in the speech of Zeresh and the wise men to Haman:* "If Mordecai be of the seed of the Jews, (the CONFESSORS-OF-JEHOVAH, for such is the interpretation of the word Judahite, or Jew,) thou wilt not prevail against him, but wilt surely fall before him." The signification of the name JACOB has been greatly obscured by our translators, through the use of the more learned term 'supplant.' "And Esau said, Is he not rightly named Jacob? these two times hath he tripped up my heels: he took away my birth-right; and now hath he taken

* Esth. vi. 13.

away my blessing." And Jacob called the name of that place PENIEL, (פניאל), and PENUEL, (פנואל), GOD-HATH-LOOKED-GRACIOUSLY: "for," said he, "I have seen God face to face, and my life has been preserved."

The subsequent history of the Edomites of the East, so far as it has been recorded, may be related in few words: we know, indeed, little more of their history* than as it is connected with that of the Jews. They were smitten by Saul, in the earlier part of his reign, or about the year 1087 before Christ.† About the year 1044 before Christ,‡ David and his captains made an entire conquest of the Edomites; slew many thousands of them; compelled the rest to become his tributaries and servants; and planted garrisons among them to secure their obedience. In this state of servitude they continued about one hundred and fifty years, or to the year before Christ 889. In the days of Jehoram, § the son of Jehoshaphat King of Judah, they revolted, and recovered their liberties, and made a king over themselves; but afterwards, Amaziah King of Judah, slew of Edom, in the Valley of Salt

* Bishop Newton on the Prophecies.

† 1 Sam. xiv. 47.

‡ 2 Sam. viii. 14; 1 Kings xi. 16; 1 Chron. xviii. 13.

§ 2 Kings viii. 20.

ten thousand, and took SELAH by war,* and called the name of it JOKTEEL: and other ten thousand, left alive, did the children of Israel carry away captive, and brought them unto the top of the rock (whereon Selah was built), and cast them down from the top of the rock, so that they were all broken in pieces.† Amaziah's son, Uzziah, took from them Elath, that commodious haven on the Red Sea, and fortified it anew,‡ and restored it to Judah. Judas Maccabeus attacked and defeated them several times;§ killing, on one occasion, no fewer than twenty thousand, and more than twenty thousand on another: he took their chief city, Hebron, and the towns thereof, and pulled down the fortress of it, and burned the towers thereof round about. At last, his nephew Hyrcanus, the son of Simon, took others of their cities, and reduced them to the necessity of embracing the religion of the Jews, or of leaving their country, and seeking new habitations elsewhere: whereupon they submitted to be circumcised; became proselytes to the Jewish creed; and were incorporated with the church and nation of the Jews.‖ They were swal-

* 2 Kings xiv. 7.

† 2 Chron. xxv. 12.

‡ 2 Kings xiv. 22.

§ 1 Macc. v. 65; 2 Macc. x. 15, 17, 18, 23.

‖ Joseph. Antiq. lib. xiii. c. 9. 1.

lowed up, and lost, partly among the Nabathean Arabs, and partly among the Jews; and the very name of Edomite was abolished, and disused, about the end of the first century after Christ. 'And where,' asks Bishop Newton, 'is the name or the nation now?' The TRADITION OF THE RABBINS bids us go west, to Italy, and find the sons of Esau; there called THE LATINS.

And here a question of the last importance presents itself to our consideration. Does the prophetic blessing pronounced by Isaac in favour of Esau and the Edomites remain to be accomplished; or, has Heaven withheld from us the testimony required to make good the proof of its fulfilment? If there were no Edomites save the Idumeans of the East, we shall be driven to the affirmation of one of these alternatives; since signal failure has attended all attempts to sustain the accomplishment of the prediction by the records of the history of the Edomites of the East. "Behold, thy dwelling shall be of the FATNESS OF THE EARTH, and of the DEW OF HEAVEN from above." "The prophecy of Malachi," says Bishop Newton, "which is commonly alleged as a proof of the barrenness of the country, is rather an argument to the contrary; for this implies that the country was fruitful before; and that its present unfruitfulness was rather an effect of war and devastation than any natural defect and failure in the soil." On the words, "AND BY THY SWORD SHALT THOU LIVE," the Bishop remarks: "Esau himself might be said to live much by the sword; for he was a cunning hunter, and man of the field; and he and his children gat possession of Mount Seir by force and violence, by destroying and expelling from thence the Horites, the former inhabitants." If we carefully examine the prophecy of Malachi, we shall be satisfied that it refers to the original sterility of Seir, and describes the condition of the country as it existed when the Almighty gave it to the Edomites. "Was not Esau Jacob's brother? saith the Lord: yet I loved Jacob and hated Esau; and I laid his mountains and his heritage waste, for the dragons of the wilderness." To say of a cunning hunter that he was a swordsman, and of a man of the field that he lived by his sword, would seem to be a perversion of language as gross as it would be to designate the battles and sieges of a Marlborough, or a Wellington, fox-huntings and battues; and the title of the children of Edom to Mount Seir was precisely that by which the sons of Israel claimed Canaan. "I gave Mount Seir unto

Esau for a possession." "As the Lord did to the children of Esau, which dwelt in Seir, when he destroyed the Horites from before them; and they succeeded them, and dwelt in their stead, even unto this day." It is not said of the Israelites, that they lived by the sword; and, therefore, something beyond the mere making of war, which is common to all nations, must have been intended by the prophet when he applied these words to the predictive history of the house of Esau. The further observation of the Bishop becomes, when opposed to the RABBINICAL TRADITION with which we have to do, a mere begging of the question. "Esau," he says, "solicited a blessing; and the author of the Epistle to the Hebrews,* tells us that Isaac blessed both Jacob and Esau: whereas, had he consigned Esau to such a barren and wretched country, it would, rather than a blessing, have been a curse." Doubtless, Esau would have preferred a more fruitful field to dwell in: nevertheless, he inhabited Mount Seir; and, so doing, obeyed the declared will of God.

But, if rejecting these, and such-like interpretations, as wholly unworthy of reception, we can assign an Idumean origin to the Latin people, we at once

* Chap. xi. 20.

discover that this great prophecy, like every other fulfilled prophecy of God, has been accomplished to the very letter, and in the fulness of the letter, of its terms. "Behold THY DWELLING shall be of the FATNESS OF THE EARTH, and of THE DEW OF HEAVEN from above." To place the reader in full possession of the glowing description of Italy given by Dionysius,* it would be necessary to transcribe nearly the whole of two of the chapters of his ROMAN ANTIQUITIES. In his opinion, Italy excelled in fertility, not merely the countries of Europe, but those of every other portion of the world; not excepting even Egypt, Libya, and Babylonia. He speaks particularly of the 'fatness of the earth,' the corn-lands, producing as much as three crops in a single year; and, as if referring to the very prophecy we are now considering, he notices the 'dew of heaven from above,' the dewiness and moisture of the herbage, which kept the cattle feeding on it always in good condition. Then, he describes the happy temperature of the climate, suiting itself to every season; so that neither the formation of fruits, nor the constitution of animals, were in the least injured by excessive

* Lib. i. cap. 36, 37.

cold or heat; and, lastly, he affirms that the plains below Alba (the central city* of the Latins), were beautiful to the eye, rich in the produce of all sorts of fruit, and in no degree inferior to the other parts of Italy. "AND BY THY SWORD SHALT THOU LIVE." The Romans were, perhaps, the very people of whom it might most justly be predicated that they 'got their living' by the sword. "War," said the elder Cato, "is the business of the Roman people." "As the Romans themselves relate," said Mithridates,† "that they were nourished by the dugs of a wolf; so all that people have the disposition of wolves, never to be satiated with blood and power, greedy and hungry after riches." And Minucius Felix:‡ "Whatever the Romans hold, cultivate, or possess, is a prey won by profligate boldness: all their temples are erected out of the ruins of cities, and the plunder of the gods." "AND THOU SHALT SERVE THY BROTHER." This portion, and only this portion of the prophecy, was certainly accomplished by the Edomite of the East. "And it shall come to pass WHEN THOU SHALT WANDER FAR AWAY, WHEN

* Strabo.

† Justin. lib. xxxviii. cap. 6.

‡ Octav. cap. xxv.

THOU SHALT HAVE THE DOMINION, that thou shalt BREAK HIS YOKE from off thy neck." To what part of the history of the Edomites, yet ascertained, will we refer these words for their fulfilment? When did Esau obtain dominion? When did he wander from Mount Seir; and whither, in his wanderings, did he go? Yet, (Rome's Idumean origin admitted,) what prophecy ever received accomplishment more literal and complete? In the destruction of Jerusalem, and the subjugation of Judæa and the Jews, this acknowledged MISTRESS OF THE NATIONS, did indeed break off the yoke imposed by Jacob on her neck.

Guided, then, by the words of Scripture, and the TRADITION OF THE RABBINS, let us now turn westward, and seek the Edomites of Isaac's prophecy on Italian ground.

* * * *

The great question which presents itself at the outset of all inquiries into the antiquities of the Roman history, is, Whether* the TROJAN LEGEND be ancient and home-sprung; or whether it originated with, and was obtained by the Romans from, the Greeks. The result of the laborious and

* Niebuhr.

most satisfactory inquiries of Niebuhr on this point may be compressed into small space. "The story," he says, "that the Trojans were not utterly destroyed at the fall of Troy, but that a part of them survived, and that this remnant had been governed by the house of Æneas, is as old as the Homeric poems. But the Trojans under Æneas, even according to the account which assigns them the greatest importance, were not an immigrating tribe, such as would alter the people it unites with. In the earliest Roman accounts, they are represented as the crew of a single ship; and even in the later narrative they are still no more than a small band, for whom the fields of a single village would suffice. But the passage in the Twentieth Book of the Iliad * would more naturally refer the prophecy to the occupation by Æneas, and the independent Dardanians, of the desolated territory of Ilium after the departure of the Greeks; and, accordingly, Aretinus of Miletus, a poet contemporary with the building of Rome, says that Æneas and his followers retired to Mount Ida. Now, if the

* For Priam, now, and Priam's faithless kind,
At length are odious to th' all-seeing mind:
On great Æneas shall devolve the reign;
And sons succeeding sons the lasting line sustain.
Pope's Iliad, Book xx., lines 353-356, and the note.

Milesian poet, whose great antiquity Dionysius of Halicarnassus expressly urges, had related anything about a subsequent emigration of Æneas, it is inconceivable that Dionysius should have rejected his evidence, when he was amassing all that he could muster out of Hellanicus, Cephalon, and other writers so much more recent. After the middle of the fifth century of Rome, Callias adopted the story of the Trojans settling in Latium, and uniting with the Aborigines, which he indicates by the marriage of Roma with King Latinus. Soon afterwards, Pyrrhus crossed over into Italy; and Pausanias* held the notion that he felt himself called upon, as a descendant of Achilles, to wage war with the Romans, as a Trojan colony; this notion being, in all probability, borrowed from some contemporary writer, Hieronymus or Timæus. From this time forward, the belief in the Trojan colony became universal amongst the Greeks: it was professed by Eratosthenes in the first half of the next century; and it is only by mere accident that we possess no Greek work in which it is expressed more ancient than the Lycophron of Cassandra, written about the year of Rome 560. Whatever

* Att. cap. 12.

use learned Romans, in the age of Augustus, might make of Greek poets, to show that the tradition was known early to the Greeks, it is extremely improbable that a belief concerning its origin, adopted by the whole nation, should have been borrowed from abroad; above all, it is improbable that a belief of this kind should be of foreign origin when recognized by the state, a state so proud, and so contemptuous towards every thing foreign, as was Rome. That it was so recognized, we find remarkable proofs, in collecting the earliest traces of the Trojan legend amongst the Romans; proofs drawn from times when Greek literature had certainly not found admission, except with a few individuals. The first transaction between the Greeks and the Romans was the application of the Roman Senate to the Ætolians for the freedom of the Acarnanians, on the plea that the Romans were bound to protect those whose ancestors alone, of all the Greeks, took no share in the war against their progenitors, the Trojans. This embassy must not be dated before the year of the city 509, nor later than 515 or 516. About the same time, the Senate wrote a letter to King Seleucus Callinicus, who reigned after the year of Rome 509, demanding, as the condition of their entering into a treaty of friendship and alliance with him, that the Ilians, the kinsmen of the Roman people, should be exempted from tribute. The Ilians were also included by the Romans in their first treaty of peace with Macedonia, in the year of the city 549. Fifteen years afterwards, when the Scipios crossed the Hellespont, the Ilians boasted of their affinity with the Romans, and called them their colony: the Romans were delighted to see their mother-country; and the consul offered sacrifice in the citadel to Athene. The appeal was dishonest: for these Ilians were originally an Æolian colony, mixed by the kings of Macedonia (who at one time enlarged the city, and at another changed its site), with a concourse of people taken out of various nations." "The Trojan legend was not brought into Latium by Greek literature; but must be considered home-sprung."

Such is the result of the inquiries and investigations of Niebuhr; and from these premises the historian draws a conclusion, the very last at which he might have been expected to arrive. "In spite," says he, "of the fact that the Trojan legend was not brought into Latium by the Greeks, but must be considered home-sprung, it has not the

SLIGHTEST FOUNDATION IN HISTORICAL TRUTH; nor has it even the slightest HISTORICAL IMPORTANCE. A belief of this sort does not require long to become a national one, in spite of the most obvious facts, and the clearest historical proofs to the contrary; and then, thousands would be ready to shed their blood for it: they that would introduce it, need but tell people roundly that it is what their forefathers knew and believed; only the belief was neglected, and sank into oblivion." Well may reasoning of this kind cause us to start.

The Trojan legend, as Niebuhr himself confesses, was a national belief; that is (for the proposition must be qualified by the testimony of Dionysius, before cited*), it was the persuasion of the great majority, though not of the entirety, of the Roman people: all concurred in deriving the origin of the nation from an Æneas; and the most part (amongst them Dionysius), held that this Æneas was the Æneas of Homer, the son of Venus and Anchises. We have here a proud and powerful people, good haters of all foreigners, giving evidence against themselves; and yet we must refuse

* Page 29.

them our belief. Nations have ever wished and tried to make themselves out aborigines, autochthones, not outcasts and defeated wanderers: but the Romans must not be listened to, when, spite of this most natural inclination, they cling to the persuasion that the founders of their race, their own Æneas and his followers, were helpless, homeless fugitives, "Cremata patria et domo* profugi, sedem, condendæque urbi locum, quærentes." "What cause," exclaims Dionysius,† "can be assigned for the monuments erected to Æneas in Italy, if he never reigned in those parts, resided there, or was entirely unknown?" And, with the Translator of the same historian, Spelman,‡ we may well retort, that to reject the tradition is 'an attempt to transform all history into romance; to destroy the use, by destroying the credit, of it; and to deprive mankind of the best guides both in public and private life, examples.'

But, let us test the credit of the legendary history of Rome by the application to it of the rules laid down by Leslie,§ and see how much it offers to us of that evidence on the faith of which even

* Liv. lib. i, c. 1. † Lib. i., cap. 54.

‡ London, 1758, vol. i., p. 216.

§ Short Method with the Deists, Lond. 1699.

miracles must be admitted and believed. The rules are: first, that the matter of fact be such, as that men's outward senses, their eyes and ears, may be the judges of it; secondly, that the fact be done publicly, in the face of the world; thirdly, that not only public monuments be kept up in memory of it, but some outward actions or observances be instituted and performed; and, fourthly, that such monuments, and such actions or observances (profess to) be instituted, and to commence from the time that the matter of fact was done. Tried by these rules, how little of the antiquities of the Roman story will remain unproved. The sacrifice yearly offered by the pontiffs and consuls to Æneas, as Jupiter Indiges; the Lupercalia; the Quirinalia; the lifting of the bride over the threshold of her husband's home; the accompanying cry, 'Talassa;' and the many other rites and outward actions observed and done in memory and attestation of the Roman legend, must be got rid of and disproved, before the story which they affirm is discarded and sentenced to oblivion, as unworthy of belief. What, too, is to become of the brazen wolf, and the cottage of Romulus, preserved to the times of Nero, if neither wolf nor Romulus were a chief actor in the tale? False relics imply true revelation, and owe their value to a confirmed belief. The pretended portions of the cross of Christ, and the Santa Casa of Loretto, pre-suppose unwavering faith in a crucified Saviour, and His virgin mother; and derive their existence solely from this creed. "No human sagacity," says Niebuhr, "can arrive at a decisive solution of the question, What, after all, can have been the origin of the tradition?": nevertheless, aided by the TRADITION OF THE RABBINS, I venture to affirm, that we may establish the certainty of Rome's legendary history by indisputable proofs.

* * * *

The pedigree of the Roman people, as found in Virgil, Livy, Dionysius, and other writers, is enveloped in as thick a darkness, and is as contradictory in itself, as that which at one time covered and distinguished the genealogy of the Roman Jupiter himself. CHAOS gave birth to NOX; from NOX came all things; the eldest of the gods was OURANOS; from Ouranos sprang CHRONOS, otherwise called SATURN; Saturn gave being to divers sons, among them, JUPITER; and JUPITER, or ZEUS, was the FATHER

BOTH OF GODS AND MEN. Such was the genealogical labyrinth in which the devout Roman was obliged to walk; and (for he had no other creed), such were the polytheistic absurdities he was content to reverence and adore. He worshipped Saturn, the father of the great Jupiter; he worshipped Jupiter's grandfather, Ouranos; he worshipped Nox, the first parent of Jupiter and the rest; he worshipped Jupiter; and him he worshipped as the FATHER OF GODS AND MEN. But LIGHT which was TO LIGHTEN THE GENTILES came from Judea; and missionaries, issuing from the Holy Land, expostulated with the heathen world, touching the absurdities and contradictions of the Gentile faith. They taught that in this their Theogony there existed but a single truth: that their ZEUS, their JUPITER, by the Jews and by Himself denominated JEHOVAH, was the ONLY GOD; that by the word of the mouth of JEHOVAH all things were created, and by the fiat of His power all things were upholden and preserved; and that He, theUncreated, Eternal, Infinite, Omnipotent, and Unchangeable, was the great AUTHOR of Chaos, and Night, and Day, and Heaven, and Earth, and Time, and Eternity, Angels, and Men, and all things else. The vaunted wisdom of the Greek stooped to be instructed by the Revelation of the Jew: the Mythology of the ancient world was thrown aside; and (so to speak) the true Theogony was established in its place. In like manner, when Virgil, Livy, and the others, affect to record the origin and genealogy of the Romans, they involve themselves in the grossest contradictions; contradictions never, I think, sufficiently noticed, at any rate, never fairly encountered and disposed of, by Beaufort, Niebuhr, or any other modern writer on the subject. At one time, and in one portion of the writings of the ancients, the whole Latin people are the descendants of Æneas and his followers; at another, and in a subsequent part of the same authors, Æneas becomes the adopted son of King Latinus, and he and his adherents are received into, and made members of the family of the Aboriginal Latins. "Genus unde Latinum, Albanique patres, atque altæ mænia Romæ," writes Virgil; and, so far, he is intelligible and consistent with himself. From Æneas, and his band of followers, came the whole Latin race: Alba and the Albans were the progenitors and head of all the other

Latin towns; and from amongst the Albans came the 'mænia Romæ;' not the inhabitants, but the builders, of great Rome. Yet, how completely is this clear and consistent account of the original of the Latins contradicted by the contents of the succeeding books of the Æneid. So Livy:* "Bellum utrimque summa ope parabatur, civili simillimum bello, prope inter parentes natosque; Trojanam utramque prolem: quum Lavinium ab Troja, ab Lavinio Alba, ab Albanorum stirpe regum oriundi Romani essent." And, again:† "Ab eo (Latino Silvio) coloniæ aliquot deductæ, PRISCI LATINI appellati." And yet it is clear, from the first chapter of Livy's history, that by the words "Latinus rex, Aboriginesque, qui tum ea tenebant loca," he intends to describe the Latin people as dwellers in Latium from time immemorial, and as, perhaps, the very Autochthones of the land. Servius is, I believe, the only writer amongst the very few that have noticed them, who has made any attempt at the reconciliation of these glaring contradictions, and the removal of these difficulties. All others seem content to take as certain the statements which make the Latins the

* Lib. i. cap. 23. † Lib. i. cap. 3.

Aborigines of Latium: but, in doing this, they appear to forget that it was incumbent on them to reconcile, if possible, the authors of these statements with themselves. The following is the commentary of Servius on the words 'genus unde Latinum,' of Virgil: "Si jam fuerunt Latini, et Latium dicebatur, contrarium est quod dicit, ab Æneа Latinos originem ducere. UNDE, adverbium est de loco; non deductio a persona. Tamen, Cato in Originibus, dicit hoc: Primo Italiam tenuisse quosdam qui appellantur Aborigines; hos postea, adventu Æneæ, Phrygibus junctos, Latinos uno nomine nuncupatos: ergo, descendunt Latini non tantum a Trojanis, sed etiam ab Aboriginibus. Est autem vera expositio hæc. Novimus qui victi, victorum nomen accipiunt. Potuit, ergo, victore Æneа, perire nomen Latinum: sed, volens sibi favorem Latii conciliare, nomen Latinum non solum illis non sustulit, sed etiam Trojanis imposuit. Merito, ergo, illi tribuit, quod in ipso fuerat ut posset perire." But the word UNDE, as an adverb of place, must, necessarily, refer the origin of the Latins to the Troy of Priam; that is, to Æneas and his followers: and Virgil makes the Trojan leader the guest, not the conqueror, of Latinus and his subjects: "Dis sedem exiguam patriis litusque rogamus innocuum, et cunctis undamque auramque patentem,"* say the Trojans, supplicating Latinus. The true reason of these contradictory accounts, as given both by Virgil and by Livy, is apparent. The current of popular belief ran so strongly in favour of the opinion which made the whole Latin people descendants of Æneas and his Trojans, and the authority of the legends in support of the same supposition was so great, that these writers were unable to oppose the two conjoined: at the same time, they could not reconcile the common story with the facts, that the very name of Trojan was no more, and that the Romans were assuredly a Latin people: wherefore, they placed both these originals before their readers, and left them to encounter the contradictions, thus created, as best they might. The possibility that the Trojans and the Latins might be one and the same people, Trojans inhabiting Latium under the name of Latins, and so giving that country its name, would seem never to have occurred, either to the ancients or the moderns. What the Jews, what the Hebrew prophets and preachers, did for the Theogony of the

* 7 Æ. 229.

Roman, they may be found capable of effecting for the Roman story; by removing this great difficulty, and so revealing the true origin of the Roman people. For, it is manifest that the tradition with which we have to do, must, if true, be referred to a higher antiquity than the days of any of those we commonly call RABBINS, and must derive its original from a far holier source. If JONATHAN BEN UZZIEL, and THE TALMUDISTS, knew the Romans to be Edomites, they had the tradition from their fathers: it must be carried, through the MEMBERS OF THE GREAT SYNAGOGUE, upward to EZRA and the later prophets, at the least; it must be referred to times when (in the language of the Greeks) the gods conversed with men, or (as the Jewish Rabbin would express it) when holy men spake as they were moved by the Spirit of God: the tradition may be as old as the Lamentations of Jeremiah; as old, perhaps, as the prophetic writings of Isaiah.* The study of Roman or Grecian archæology, would find no favour with the Rabbins of whom we speak. To them, the wisdom of the Greeks, mixed as it was with its absurd polytheism, was foolishness, to be detested;

* Isa. lxiii. 1.

Rome, where the congregated gods of all the GOYIM jostled each other, and fought for rank and room, was, to these men, the mother of abominations, and the cage of every unclean thing. Wherefore, as the tradition, if true, must have a Divine origin; so will its truth be discoverable by the application of it to the elucidation of the legendary history of Rome. And, to this I now proceed.

* * * *

Esau and Jacob spake the same language, the Hebrew of Moses and the prophets; and this tongue was also spoken, in all its purity, by the sons of Jacob, as late, at least, as the destruction of the First Temple, or for more than one hundred and sixty years after the foundation of Rome. The same language may, therefore, have been found with the children of Esau during the like period; and a very strong presumption (to say no more), that they also spoke the Biblical Hebrew, arises from the fact, that the few names of places and persons found in their history (as Selah, Bozrah, Job and his friends, and others) are all Hebrew. Now, divested of their classical terminations, the names ÆNEAS, Saturnia, Latini, Latium, TROJA, Lavinium, Alba Longa, ROMA, Ascanius, Silvius, Rhea Silvia, ROMULUS, Remus, LUPERCUS, Numa Pompilius, Tarquinius Priscus, DEUS, JUPITER, JOVIS, Janus, Semo Sancus, Jupiter Latiaris, Jupiter Feretrius, Jupiter Stator, Quirinus, Saturnalia, Quirinalia, Luperca, Lupercal, Lupercalia, Palilia, Consualia, Templum, Altar, Ara, Sacerdos, Flamen, CAPITOLIUM, Tarpeia, Rex, Tribus, Ramnes, Titienses, Luceres, Pater, Senator, Patricius, Plebs, Patronus, Cliens; all these names, and almost all the other names, whether of person, place, or occupation, we meet with in the legendary history of Rome, are HEBREW: they are all of them significant in the HEBREW TONGUE; they tell the tale of Rome; and (being witnesses above suspicion), they avouch its truth. And the tale they tell runs (briefly) thus. ENIIAH, also called SATURNIIAH, and his followers, were foreigners and fugitives; they fled from fire, and sword, and bonds, and hid themselves in Italy; they spoke the HEBREW TONGUE; calling themselves LATINIM, HIDING-(or HIDDEN-)ONES, in LATION, LATIUM, LATLAND, LAND-OF-THE-HIDER, they set up their rest; they brought with them the RELIGION OF THE PATRI-

ARCHS; they worshipped the ALMIGHTY by His great name JEHOVAH, JHOVAH, JHOVIH, JOVIS; the God who had redeemed them from the house of bondage, and made freemen of them in Italia, they invoked by the name יְהוֹ־פִּטֵּר, JEHOPITTER, JOPITTER, (by subsequent corruption) JUPITER, JEHOVAH - (THAT) - HATH - SET-FREE, JEHOVAH-THE-ENFRANCHISER; like the Israelites in Egypt, they mixed not with the idolaters about them; like the sons of Jacob, from a small band (some seventy, or a hundred persons), they grew into a nation, and became THE LATIN PEOPLE; they first built a little town, which they named TROIAH, and so were called TROIANIM; they styled themselves LAVINIM, ADHERENTS, as well as Latins, and the next town they built they called LAVINION, DWELLING-PLACE-OF-THE-LAVINES; Troiah being abandoned for Lavinium, the name Trojan ceased, and was found no more: under Eniiah, Ascani, and the Silvian kings, these Latins led a peaceful, virtuous, godly, happy, life; this was the GOLDEN AGE of Italy; these the SATURNIA REGNA, not of the fabled Saturn, but of God's saint SATURNIIAH, good ENIIAH; RHEA

SILVIA, SIGHTLY SILVIA, gave birth to the twin brothers, ROMULUS AND REMUS; and the shepherd ROMULUS, in his youth, and by his shepherd comrades, called LUPERCUS, WOLF-PRESERVED, built ROME.

Such is the substance of the first part of my argument; an outline of the testimony to the truth of the TRADITION OF THE RABBINS obtainable from an ANALYSIS OF THE OLDEST LATIN. It has next to be expanded and enforced.

* * * *

Jacob and Esau spoke the Hebrew of Moses and the prophets: but was the Biblical Hebrew the mother-tongue of Abraham also? Was it the language brought by the patriarch with him to Canaan, or that found by him on his arrival there; the language of the Canaanites, or Phœnicians, then the inhabitants of the promised land? TEN VERSES (not interpreted) preserved in the PŒNULUS* of PLAUTUS, contained an answer to this question; and, in the year 1850, I obtained from them a text differing but little from the Hebrew of King David and the Books of Kings, and pointed in conformity with the Masoretic punctuation of those books.

* Act v. sc. 1, (Hanno loq.) NYTH ALONIM, &c,

This exposition of the Ten Verses, published in a tract of fifteen pages, is too long to be inserted here; but, as it forms an important step in my argument (and as no copies of the book are now obtainable), I will annex it, by way of Appendix, to the present volume. It proves, if admitted, the identity of the Phœnician with the Hebrew of the Bible; it shows that the HOLY TONGUE must, like the HOLY LAND, have been derived to the chosen seed through Ham's accursed son, Canaan; and that the sacred text of Moses and the prophets is Phœnician, expressed in the Chaldaic character, which character may, perhaps, have been brought by Abraham from Ur of the Chaldees. If, now, we find the descendants of the Phœnician Dido speaking, in the days of Plautus, the Hebrew of the Israelitish kings, we have strong reasons for believing that the language of the Edomites, when the Trojan Æneas is thought to have fled to Italy, was Hebrew also, or a dialect next door to it. And this supposition receives great support from the fact, that most of the few names of persons and places found in the Scripture history of the Idumeans are clearly Hebrew. Thus: SELAH, Rock; BOZRAH, (perhaps) IMPREGNABLE;

JOB, PERSECUTED-ONE; ELIPHAZ, MY-GOD-PURIFIETH; ZOPHAR, HASTENER; ELIHU, HE-IS-MY-GOD, or GOD-IS-MY-GOD, are all Phœnician, or Hebrew-appellations. But if, with many of the most learned, we suppose the Book of Job to have been written by an Idumean, we at once end the question, and establish the fact. However, it is unnecessary to pursue the subject further, since it is quite sufficient, for our present purpose, to show that the Edomites would very probably speak the Hebrew, whilst they cannot be proved to have spoken any other tongue. That HEBREW was the LANGUAGE of the OLDEST LATINS, will shortly be made apparent; but this will not suffice to prove the Latins to be Edomites. They may have been Canaanites, Israelites, or some other people speaking the Phœnician tongue; and the fact that they were in truth Idumeans, can be established by the evidence of prophecy alone.

"There is no part of the verbal criticism of the HEBREW TEXT," says Gesenius, "which opens to us so wide a field as the PROPER-NAMES; they belong to the small store of Hebrew which has been handed down to us; and the existence of many a root is further confirmed by means of them." This learned Hebraist might have added, that the PROPER-NAMES frequently form a commentary on the history of Scripture, and may be applied by us both in support of the sacred story, and of ancient traditions existing by the side of the inspired text. And these names derive their explanatory powers chiefly from the fact that, whilst they are in themselves significant, they speak the language of the person by whom they are imposed, not of the party on whom they are impressed; the language of the parents who give, not that of the children who receive them. Thus, when God names the chosen seed of Abraham, it is the Almighty Himself who speaks. And thou shalt call his name ISAAC, יִצְחָק, HE-SHALL-LAUGH.* So Hannah: she prayed for a child, and the Lord granted her petition;† wherefore she called his name SAMUEL, שְׁמוּעָה־אֵל, HEARD-OF-GOD, HEARKENED-TO-BY-GOD; thereby proclaiming, that she, Hannah, had been listened to, on this occasion, by the Lord. So

* Gen. xxv. 11; xxvi. 3, 12, 13, 14, 16, 24, 28. Joseph. Antiq. lib. i. cap. 18, 3.

† 1 Sam. i. 27.

the name of David's successor in the throne, SOLOMON, שְׁלֹמֹה, SHELOMOH, is an appellation formed from the participle שָׁלוּם, SHALUM, and the pronoun הוּא, HU, HE. It is the language of David, and it signifies, PACIFIED-(IS)-HE; that is, the Almighty, who had pardoned the sins of David, committed in the murder of Uriah, and his adultery with Uriah's wife. But the great importance of this property of the HEBREW PROPER-NAMES will be best established by the application of it to a very ancient tradition of the Jews. We read that on the death of Jehoiakim, King of Judah,* "Jehoiakin his son reigned in his stead, and did that which was evil in the sight of the Lord, according to all that his father had done." He was, however, wise enough 'to go out to the king of Babylon;' and thereby brought himself within the promise made by Jeremiah; he received 'his own life for his portion of the spoil' of Jerusalem, and was carried captive by Nebuchadnezzar to Babylon, instead of being put to death. In the thirty-seventh year of his captivity, Evil-Merodach lifted up the head of Jehoiakin out of prison, and spake kindly to him; he changed his prison gar-

* 2 Kings xxiv. 6.

ments, and set up his throne above the throne (rather, set his seat at table above the seats) of the kings that were with him at Babylon; and he did eat bread continually before (in the presence of) the King of Babylon, all the days of his life." Now, the Jews possess a tradition that this Jechoniah repented him of his sins, and so obtained mercy with God. He had a son, called in the Old Testament SHEALTIEL, in the New, SALATHIEL; the father of that Zerubbabel, or Sheshbazzar, who became the leader of a portion of the Jews restored to Jerusalem by virtue of the edict issued by Cyrus, in the first year of his reign. SHEALTIEL, שְׁאַלְתִּיאֵל, signifies, I-HAVE-SOUGHT-GOD; and SALATHIEL, שַׁלְתִּיאֵל, may be translated, GOD-HAS-DRAWN-ME-OUT; to wit, out of my dungeon. We have, I imagine, in these names, most interesting evidence of the certainty of the Jewish tradition touching this Jechoniah; and we may well accept the assurance they offer us, that this wicked man did, indeed, turn away from his wickedness, and (by the mercy of God), save his soul alive.* In both the appellations given by him to his son, Jechoniah speaks

* Gen. xxxvi. 38.

to his posterity through the child; he testifies his repentance, and receives the favour of Evil-Merodach as the gift of God.

Some rules observable in the formation of the PROPER-NAMES of Scripture will next require our attention.

And, FIRST. By a beautiful idiom of the Hebrew, events decreed by the Almighty, and, therefore, certainly to come to pass, are commonly treated, both by Himself and by his creatures, as having actually taken place; so that, in the great majority of cases, the future of prophecy (or certainty) will be expressed by the past tense of the Hebrew verb. The phraseology found in the text next cited runs through all the books of the Old Testament. "It is a light thing that thou shouldst be my servant, to raise up the tribes of Jacob, and to restore the preserved of Israel; I WILL ALSO GIVE (literally, I HAVE ALSO GIVEN) thee for a light unto the Gentiles." * This form of speaking should seem to have originated with the Great Disposer of Events, and is referred to by St. Paul, in his Epistle to the Romans.† "Therefore is it, that it (the promise) is of faith, that it might be by grace:

* Isa. xlix. 6. † Rom. iv. 16.

to the end the promise might be sure to all the seed; not to that only which is of the law, but to that, also, which is of the faith of Abraham; who before (in the eyes of, κατεναντι,) Him whom he believed, God, WHO QUICKENETH THE DEAD, AND CALLETH THOSE THINGS WHICH BE NOT AS THOUGH THEY WERE, is the Father of us all (the Great Patriarch both of believing Jews and Gentiles): as it is written, A father of many nations HAVE I MADE thee." God, naming Abraham, and making him the father of many nations, used the past tense of the verb; and thereby (writes the Apostle), the Almighty quickened the dead, assured the Patriarch of his resurrection from the dead, and treated the future people as already born. ABRAHAM, says St. Jerome, signifies PATER-VIDENS-POPULUM; literally, PATER-(QUI)-VIDIT-POPULUM; the Patriarch that has beheld, the Patriarch that shall assuredly behold, the "great multitude which no man can number, out of all nations, and kindreds, and people, and tongues," hereafter to stand "before the throne, and before the Lamb, clothed with white robes, and with palms in their hands." The name Abraham is compounded of אָב, AB, FATHER, PATRIARCH;

רָאָה, RAAH, HE HAS SEEN; and עָם, AM, PEOPLE: אַב־רָאָה־עָם, AB-RAAH-AM, אַבְרָהָם ABRAHAM: THE-PATRIARCH-THAT-HAS-BEHELD-THE-PEOPLE; THE-PATRIARCH-THAT-SHALL-ASSUREDLY-BEHOLD-THE-PEOPLE. And the fulfilment of God's promise, so far as it respects the resurrection of Abraham from the dead, is solemnly asserted by our Lord himself. "Your father Abraham rejoiced, *ἵνα ἴδῃ*, ut videret, because he was to see, my day: *και εἰδεν, και ἐχαρη*, et vidit, et gavisus est; and he has seen it, and is glad."*

SECONDLY. In the formation of a proper-name, and for the purpose of distinguishing the name itself from the phrase out of which it is formed, a vowel will commonly be changed. Thus, from יִצְחַק, ITSKHĂK, we have יִצְחָק, ITSKHĀK, ISAAC, HE-SHALL-LAUGH; from אֶלִי־שָׁמַע, ELI-SHAMĂ, אֱלִישָׁמָע, ELISHAMĀ, MY-GOD-HATH-HEARD; from אֶלִי־שָׁבַע, ELI-SHĀBA, the feminine אֱלִישֶׁבַע, ELISHĔBA, MY-GOD-HATH-SWORN; from יִשְׂרֶה־אֵל, ISRĔ-EL, יִשְׂרָאֵל, ISRĀEL (AS)-GOD-SHALL-HE-WRESTLE; from יְהוֹ־אוֹדֶה, JEHO-ODĔH, JEHOODĔH, יְהוּדֶה, JEHUDĔH, יְהוּדָה,

* John viii. 56.

JEHUDĀH, JUDĀH, JEHOVAH-WILL-I-CONFESS, CONFESSOR-OF-JEHOVAH. And so on.

THIRDLY. No proper-name is ever formed by the subtraction from its forming phrase of any of the pure consonants; that is to say, any of the letters of the Hebrew alphabet except the six VOCALES LITERÆ (as Jerome calls* them); ALEPH, HE, VAU, KHETH, YOD, and AYIN. These letters, called by the Jews (speaking of four of them), MATRES (or MATRICES) LECTIONIS, are vowels† as well as consonants; consonants holding within them, as in wombs or moulds, the vowel sounds of the language, and being used sometimes as consonants, sometimes as vowels. The Vocales Literæ, with their vowel-points, will frequently be expelled from the text, in the formation of a proper-name; but no one of the pure consonants is ever thus excluded from the appellation. A single instance will suffice. There is scarcely, I believe, a Hebraist who will not deduce the name JOHN from the Hebrew יְחָנָן, JOCHANAN, JEHOVAH-WILL-BE-GRACIOUS.‡ But the omission of the final NUN, (N),

* De Nominibus Hebraicis, &c.

† Joseph. Bell. Jud. v. c. 5, 7.

‡ First Rule.

in the Greek Ιωαννης, is fatal to this derivation. JOCHANAN was a very common name amongst the Jews, and is always written, in the Greek of the Septuagint translators, Ιωαναν. The Greek Ιωαννης is the Hebrew יְהוֹ־עַנֶּה; formed (as SHĂB-BĀTH from SHĀBĂTH) by the duplication of the middle consonant, the change, before the doubling-dagesh, of the first Kamets into Pathach, and of the second into Segol (second rule), as the sign of the masculine noun: יְהוֹ־עַנֶּה JEHOANNEH, JOANNEH, JEHOVAH-WILL*-BEGIN-TO-SPEAK. "But thou,† Bethlehem Ephrathah (thou, Bethlehem-that-shalt-bring-forth), out of thee shall He come forth unto me that is to be Ruler in Israel. Therefore will He give them up (will speak to them neither by Urim and Thummim, nor by prophets, nor by dreams), until the time that she which travaileth (that Bethlehem-Rachel) shall bring forth." "And ‡ they made signs to his father, how he would have him called; and he asked for a writing-table, and wrote, saying, his name is JOHN. And they marvelled all. And his mouth was opened immediately; and he was filled with the Holy Ghost, and prophesied." Well did the Angel

* First Rule. † Mic. v. 2. ‡ Luke i. 62.

Gabriel announce that, with the circumcision of the Baptist JEHOVAH WOULD BEGIN TO SPEAK; for, even the BENEDICTUS of ZACHARIAS contains an amount of prediction worthy of the chiefest of the prophets.

FOURTHLY. In the formation of a proper-name, the order of the component words will frequently, as in our own and other languages, be inverted. Thus, the Greek Ὁ-ποιος-των-μαχαιρων, A-maker-of-swords, is expressed, both in Greek and English, by a single word: Μαχαιροποιος, SWORD-MAKER. And so in the Hebrew, יְהוּדָה, JEHUDAH, is אודה־יהוה, and from אוֹדֶה אֶת־יְהוָֹה, Leah forms the name יהוּדָה, יְהוּדָה, יְהוֹ־אוֹדֶה, JEHUDA. So, יְהוֹאָשׁ, יוֹאָשׁ, JEHOASH, JOASH, is אֵשׁ־יְהוָֹה, LIGHT-(or LAMP)-OF-JEHOVAH.*

FIFTHLY. In Greek and Latin, the final H of the Hebrew will commonly be represented by Σ, or S; which letters, in such case, are mute. Thus, the names of the fourth son of Leah, and of the betrayer of our Lord, are identical; and each of them (JUDAH and JUDAS,) is to be pronounced JUDA. This silent S is supposed to have been derived to the Greeks and Latins from the Sanscrit, in which

* 1 Kin. xv. 4, and Third Rule.

language the sibilant is usually softened into H, by VISARGAH;* and it prevails, to a great extent, in the modern French, which seems to have obtained it from the Latin. At first sight, it may not appear easy to establish the identity of the Latin JOVIS and the Hebrew JĔHOVAH: but if we pronounce this name (the S being softened as in the Sanscrit), JOVIH, and reflect that the first vowel of the Hebrew word is short, so that the name readily becomes a dissyllable, JHOVIH, and, further, that with the Latins A is constantly changed into I, we shall find that JOVIS is readily deducible from the JEHOVAH, or JHOVAH, of the Jews.

SIXTHLY. The HE and YOD, or E and I, of the Hebrew, and the E and I of the Latins, have each the sound of our own E, the first of these letters being twice as long as the other of them. Nothing, I apprehend, can be more certain than that the I, as sounded in the English FIRE, has no existence either in the Hebrew, the Greek, or the Latin, when properly pronounced. Indeed, the form of the 'vowel-point' applied by the Punctionists to the Hebrew of the Bible will go far to establish the fact. For, if in the Hebrew, אִישׁ,

* Wilkins, Sanscrit Gram. pp. 12, 63.

ISH, the KHIRIK is to be pronounced as an E, then the form of the TSERE, in אֵשׁ. ESH, gives a vowel of the same sound, but of twice the length of the first. The modern Jews, indeed, pronounce the TSERE as the French E, in the words PÈRE, and MÈRE; but this seems to be a corruption of the true and ancient pronunciation of the letter; and it was, perhaps, obtained by them from the Greeks: for we find that, in the days of Plato, the Greek ETA had the sound of the English A in PAIN; whilst the earlier pronunciation* of this letter was EE. Traces of the corruption appear in the Greek translation of the Old Testament; in which the INITIAL SHEVA (or SHORT E) of the Hebrew is commonly turned into an A: as SAMUEL for SHEMUEL.

SEVENTHLY. The SHIN, or SH, of the Hebrew was unknown both to the Latins and Greeks; and this letter is always represented, both in Greek and Latin, by the unaspirated S; as SAMUEL for SHAMUEL. We find, indeed, that a large proportion even of the Hebrews were unable to articulate this letter, saying SIBBOLETH for SHIBBOLETH.

* Prof. Black, On the Pronunciation of the Greek Language.

EIGHTHLY. The Hebrews sometimes write the same word with a final HE, or H, and also with a final KHETH, or KH; as קָשָׁה and קָשַׁח, KASHAH and KASHAKH, To be hard; גָּבָה and גָּבַח, GABAH and GABAKH, To be high. On the contrary, an INITIAL KHETH will often, in Greek and Latin, be expressed by an H, or will become altogether mute: as, Ἑρμων, and Hermon, for KHERMON; Ἀννα, and Anna, for KHANNAH.

NINTHLY, and LASTLY. It has been well observed,* that "if it were necessary to describe, in one sentence, the genius and constitution of the Latin tongue, this could not be better done than by defining it to be a language which is always yearning after contraction;" further, that "the cause is to be sought in the strength and prominence of the single accent, which is generally thrown forward as far as possible;" and that "the hasty pronunciation of the Romans, so far as it was exhibited in the written forms of the language, appears chiefly in the omission of syllables in the middle of the words." Now, these are the distinguishing characteristics of the Hebrew also. Few words in that language contain more than three syllables, one of which will

* Donaldson, Varronianus, p. 269.

be shortened; an effort will commonly be made to reduce three syllables into two; and this by the suppression of the middle syllable of the word. Thus, from DĀBĀR (a word), is formed the plural DĔBĀRĪM, (not DĀBĀRĪM); and this plural, when in apposition with another noun, is reduced to a word of two syllables, DIBRĒ (not DĔBĀRĪM) KOHELETH, THE WORDS OF THE PREACHER. So, from MĔLĔK (a king), comes the feminine MALKÂH, for MĔLĔKAH; the tone accent falling almost always on the last syllable.

* * * *

To understand the history of ÆNEAS and his companions, considered as the EDOMITES of the TRADITION OF THE RABBINS, and as it is exhibited in the names occurring in the oldest Latin, it will be necessary to review the leading particulars of that system of revealed religion hereinbefore denominated THE RELIGION OF THE PATRIARCHS.

And the old fathers worshipped the ONE TRUE GOD by His name יהוה.* This name the Hebrews for several centuries before the Christian era refused, and still refuse (or, rather, have been

* Gen. xx. 4. Job i. 21. Numb. xxii. 8, 13, 19; xxiii. 3, 8, 12; xxiv. 11, 13. Cic. De Re Pub. lib. i. p. 37 (edit. Heinrich).

forbidden),* to pronounce; and Saint Jerome (who had his Hebrew from the Jewish doctors), writes thus† concerning it: "Prius nomen Domini apud Hebræos quatuor literarum est: י (Iod), ה (He), ו (Vau), ה (He); quod proprium Dei vocabulum sonat, et legi potest IEHOVA, et Hebræi *αρρητον*, id est ineffabile, opinantur." The great majority of Hebraists, following the opinion of the Jews, suppose that the true pronunciation of the Divine name has, in consequence, been lost; and that the vowel-points attached to it in the Masoretic copies of the Hebrew Scriptures belong to the words ADONAI, and ELOHIM. But, though the Jews for יְהֹוָה, JEHOVAH, substitute, on most occasions, אֲדֹנָי, ADONAI, and, in some cases, to prevent the repetition of ADONAI, אֱלֹהִים, ELOHIM, it does not follow that the true punctuation of יהוה has not been preserved, and is not actually exhibited to us by the pointing יְהֹוָה. First, because the name ADONAI being read by a CONSTANT (or IMPLIED) KERI, it would be sufficient to change the points of יהוה in those cases only where the word ELOHIM was to be used in the place of ADONAI, or where the punctuation of ADONAI was affected

* Joseph. Antiq. lib. ii. 12. 4. † On Psa. viii.

by prefixes. Next, because the points actually affixed to יהוה are not those proper to אדני, but differ from them in an important particular, the use of the SHEVA NA (or SHORT E), for the KHATEPH-PATHACH (or SHORT A), of ADONAI. Further, because the two first points attached to the Divine name occur in a very great proportion of Hebrew proper-names, as JEHONATHAN, JEHOSHAPHAT; in which it is universally admitted that the syllables JEHO represent the peculiar name of THE DEITY, and that the names themselves are properly translated by us JEHOVAH-HATH-GIVEN, JEHOVAH-HATH-JUDGED. And, lastly, because the signification attributed by the Almighty to the name יהוה leads to the punctuation found in the Masoretic text, and the pronunciation JEHOVAH. "And Moses said unto God, Behold, when I am come unto the children of Israel, and shall say unto them, The God of your fathers hath sent me unto you; and they shall say to me, WHAT IS HIS NAME? what shall I say unto them? And God said unto Moses, EHEYÈH ASHÈR EHEYÈH, I SHALL BE THAT I SHALL BE, I MUST BE THAT I MUST BE; and He said, Thus shalt thou say unto the children of Israel, EHEYÈH, I-(THAT)-MUST-BE, hath sent me unto you. And God said moreover unto Moses, Thus shalt thou say unto the children of Israel, יְהֹוָה, JEHOVAH, HE-(THAT)-MUST-BE, the God of your fathers, the God of Abraham, the God of Isaac, and the God of Jacob, hath sent me unto you: this is MY NAME for ever, and this is MY MEMORIAL unto all generations."* Now, the future of the verb הָיָה, HAYAH, TO BE, in the intensive form, and pointed as a proper-name, will give the punctuation יְהֹוָה, and the signification HE-(THAT)-SHALL-BE, HE-(THAT)-MUST-BE. For the final letter of this verb, the H, will not be doubled (as in other words in the Piel future), but the duplication will be transferred to the preceding Vau, and the form will be יְהוֹוֶה, JEHOVEH; and this future, by the change of SEGOL into KAMETS, as the sign of the proper-name,† will become יְהֹוָה, JEHOVAH. From JEHOVAH we have the contracted forms יְהוֹ, JEHO, יוֹ, JO, and יָהּ, JAH;‡ the last being written by the Greeks (with their silent S) IAS, and by the Latins IA, the pronunciation in both cases being YA. JAHU, YAHU, (יָהוּ), is compounded of יָהּ, and

* Exod. iii. 14, 15. † Second Rule. ‡ Psa. lxviii. 4.

הוּא; and is used at the end of a proper-name, to give emphasis to the appellation: as, אֵלִיָּה, ELIJAH, ELIYAH, MY-GOD-IS-JEHOVAH; אֵלִיָּהוּ, ELIJAHU, JEHOVAH-HE-IS-MY-GOD. And from the inquiry of Moses, "When they shall say unto me, What is His name, what shall I answer them?" and from a subsequent passage in Exodus,* "By my name JEHOVAH was I not known to them," it has been supposed that the INCOMMUNICABLE NAME was first assumed by the Almighty when He spoke to Moses from the burning bush. But the supposition is perfectly incompatible with the fact, that the appellation enters into the composition of the names of persons existing long before the times of Moses. Thus, JUDAH, as we have seen, signifies JEHOVAH-WILL-I-CONFESS, and is so interpreted by Leah; and JOSEPH, the name of Rachel's eldest son, is JEHOVAH-HATH-ADDED, JEHOVAH-WILL-SURELY-ADD. She called his name JOSEPH, יְהוֹ־הוֹסִיף, JEHO-HOSIPH, יְהוֹ־הוֹסֵף, JEHO-HOSEPH, יְהוֹסֵף, JEHOSEPH,† יוֹסֵף, JOSEPH; "for she said, Jehovah will add to me another son."‡ So

* Chap. vi. ver. 3. † Psa. lxxxi. 5 (6).

‡ Gen. xxx. 24. Joseph. Antiq. lib. i. cap. xix. 8.

JOCHEBED is יְהוֹ־כָבֵד, JEHO-CHABED, JEHOVAH-HATH-PRESSED-SORE, THE-HAND-OF-JEHOVAH-IS-HEAVY; and the name was, no doubt, imposed by the parents of the mother of Moses on their child in the days when the kings of Egypt made the lives of the Israelites bitter with hard bondage. Moses, then, can only be understood as asking whether the Hebrews should still continue to address the God of their fathers by His ancient name, or whether the Almighty would at that time reveal Himself to them by some other appellation, or some addition to the name JEHOVAH. In answer to the inquiry, God expounds the name; and shows that it is proper to Himself alone, INCOMMUNICABLE, and incapable of application to any other. All other beings may or may not be, for their existence depends on the Creator; of Him only can it be truly predicated, HE MUST BE. And hence we may, perhaps, interpret the more difficult text, "By my name JEHOVAH was I not known to them;" that is, was I not comprehended by them. For he is said in Scripture to be ignorant of that which He does not fully understand. "And this saying* was hid from them, neither knew they the

* Luke xviii. 34.

things that were spoken:" "For as yet they knew not the Scripture, that He must rise from the dead."* In both cases the disciples knew the words, but lacked the comprehension of them. And so it must ever be with the Divine name JEHOVAH. We may be capable of analyzing it; and, interpreting it by the rules of grammar, we may say that it signifies HE-THAT-MUST-BE: but neither man nor angel can go further; for the name involves the knowledge of the mode of the Divine existence, comprehensible by God alone: I-MUST-BE, is the utmost DEITY can reveal; HE-MUST-BE, all that man can comprehend, concerning it. And the patriarchs, thus believing and worshipping, received from God the end of their faith, even the salvation of their souls. CHRIST was with this church as He was afterwards with the church in the wilderness; THE LAMB SLAIN FROM THE FOUNDATION OF THE WORLD was with the WHOLE-BURNT-OFFERING,† and through that sacrifice, as the sacramental mean, was made unto them wisdom, and justification, and sanctification, and redemption; they were made sons of God by adoption; they

* John xx. 9.

† Job i. 5; xlii. 8. Numb. xxiii. 1, 14, 29, 30.

walked religiously in good works; * and they died in sure and certain hope of the RESURRECTION UNTO LIFE, † promised by the Almighty from the beginning of the world. ‡

* * * *

THE TRADITION OF THE RABBINS makes the ÆNEAS of the Roman story an Idumean; and the inhabitants of the East insist that JOB was a descendant of Isaac's eldest son. JOB was perfect and upright, one that feared God and eschewed evil; and the piety and righteousness of ÆNEAS are prominent features of the Roman legend: "PIUS ÆNEAS:" "Insignis PIETATE vir:" "Rex, QUO JUSTIOR ALTER, nec pietate fuit, nec bello major et armis." Job worshipped God § by His name JEHOVAH, and the appellation ÆNEAS bears testimony to the religion of the father who imposed it on his son: עין־י־יה, AYIN-I-JAH; עיניה, ENIJAH; ‖ JEHOVAH-(IS)-MY-FOUNTAIN. "Thy mercy, O JEHOVAH, is in

* Gen. xxxix. 9. Job xxix. 11–17.

† Job xiv. 12, 14, 15. Psa. xlix. 14, 15. Acts xxiii. 6; xxiv. 15. Heb. xi. 19, 35.

‡ Luke i. 69, 70. Heb. ii. 14. Jude 6, 14.

§ Job i. 21.

‖ Eniyah.

the heavens;* Thy faithfulness reacheth unto the clouds: with Thee is the fountain of life." That in flying to Italy, ÆNEAS was χρηματισθεις,† is expressly asserted by the legend. "The reason (writes Dionysius),‡ why the Trojan fleet sailed no further into Europe, is to be attributed to the oracles, and to the will of heaven, many ways revealed to them." In particular, the ship in which Æneas sailed is said to have been built for him by MERCURIUS, also called HERMES, the messenger of the gods. Now, in Jewish phraseology, even the unanimated agencies of nature are denominated ANGELS or MESSENGERS of Jehovah, when employed in the execution of the decrees of God. "He § maketh the winds His angels, and His ministers the fiery flame:" and so the tradition of the Jews recognizes the lightning of heaven as the ANGEL OF JEHOVAH by whom the host of Sennacherib the Assyrian was destroyed. The story places the arrival of Æneas in Italy, and the building of the Laurentine Troy, three hundred and thirty-three years prior to the date commonly assigned to the foundation of Rome, or in the year

* Psa. xxxvi. 5, 9.
† Matt. 11. 22.
‡ Lib. i. c. 55.
§ Psa. civ. 4.

before Christ one thousand and eighty-six. Saul, according to the Biblical chronology, ascended the throne of Israel in the year one thousand and ninety-five before Christ; and the Edomites were smitten by him in the earlier part of his reign. The utter destruction of the Amalekites by Saul must be placed some years after his victory over the Idumeans,* according to our Bible, about the year before Christ one thousand and seventy-nine. If, then, we can conceive an Idumean Æneas flying from Edom to escape the wrath of God, to avoid a destruction similar to that soon to be poured out on Amalek, and then on Edom, he might well, using the language of the Hebrews, declare himself impelled to flight by an angel of God, MERCURY or HERMES. For in the Hebrew (more properly, in the mouth of an Edomite, the Phœnician) tongue, MĖRĔC-UR (מֶרֶךְ־אוּר), by contraction † MERCUR, would signify FEAR-OF-FIRE; and חֵרֶם־אֵשׁ, KHEREM - ESH, contracted into KHERMESH, KHERMES, HERMES,‡ is the DOOM-OF-FIRE, the CURSE-OF-EXTERMINATION, pronounced by the Almighty against those sinners the Ama-

* 1 Sam. xiv. 47, 48; xv. 1, 15, 18.

† Rule Nine, p. 71. ‡ Rule Eight, p. 70.

lekites, and by virtue of which men and beasts were to be put to the sword, and the cities, and all things found therein, utterly destroyed by fire.

But the tradition preserved by Varro assigns another angel to Æneas for a guide. "Ex* quo de Troja est egressus Æneas, Veneris ille per diem quotidie stellam vidit, donec ad agrum Laurentem veniret; in quo eam non vidit ulterius: qua re et terras cognovit esse fatales." If for TROJA, in this passage, we substitute EDOM, and for STELLA VENERIS, STAR OF JEHOVAH, we behold Æneas brought to Italy by the 'leading of a star,' even as the wise men of the East, long ages afterwards, followed a like guide, "till it came and stood still over where the young child was." And this tradition, grossly perverted, appears in other writers of the Roman story, who cause Æneas to recognise the TERRÆ FATALES, the land assigned him for his dwelling-place, by the appearance of a WHITE SOW. "A SOW† beneath an oak shall lie along; ALL WHITE herself, and WHITE her thirty young. When thirty rolling years have run their race, thy son, Ascanius, on

* Servius on Æn. i. 382; ii. 801.

† Æn. viii. 61 (Dryden's translation).

this empty space, shall build a royal town of lasting fame; which from this omen shall receive its name." PORCA ALBA, translated from the Latin of Virgil into our own tongue, must certainly be rendered by the words WHITE SOW; but in the Phœnician spoken, as we assume, by Æneas the Edomite, these words would have a very different signification. In that language, POREK, with the emphatic ה, and by contraction פֹּרְקָה, PORĔKA, PORCA, joined with עַל, AL, and בָּא, BA, PORCA-AL-BA, must be rendered, THE - RESCUER - OVERHEAD - GOING; and the WHITE SOW becomes identical with the GUIDING STAR of Varro. Lycophron* changes the colour of this sow to BLACK, and calls her Συς Κελαινη; which appellation, however, contains the same idea, and refers itself to the same tradition: for PORCA NIGRA (פֹּרְקָה נִגְרָה) will signify THE-RESCUER-THE-DRAWER-OUT; THE-RESCUER-BY-DRAWING-OUT.

And here we stand on holy ground. The Roman story takes its commencement in a marvel; a miracle worthy the long series of prophecy in the accomplishment of which Æneas was to act so great a part. By the professors of that Rationalism (falsely so called),

* Cassan. ver. 1256.

which regards with equal eye the miracles of Moses, and the marvels of modern magic, the tradition will be scoffed at, and rejected: to the disciples of a wiser creed we may say (with the Apostle), That God is not the God of the Jew only, but of the Gentile also; and (with the Evangelist), That he was worthy for whom the Almighty should do this. Perhaps it is possible to carry the tradition one step higher; and, from God's doings with the patriarchs of old, derive additional interest to the tale. "It came to pass,* when God destroyed the cities of the plain, that God remembered Abraham; and (by the guidance of His angels) sent Lot out of the midst of the overthrow, when He overthrew the cities in the which Lot dwelt." And so, when the indignation of the Lord was to be poured out on Edom, may not the faith and the works of another of His servants have come up in memorial before God; and may not the Almighty, by the leading of His star, have drawn this very ÆNEAS out of Idumea in remembrance, and as a descendant, of the PATRIARCH JOB? Certain it is that the author (whoever he was), of the ORIGO GENTIS ROMANÆ has connected the name of the perfect man of Uz with the

* Gen. xix. 29.

history of Rome. Speaking of the successor of Æneas, he says, "Latini Ascanium, OB INSIGNEM VIRTUTEM, non solum Jove ortum crediderunt; sed etiam, per diminutionem, declinato paululum nomine primo, JOBUM, dein postea Iulum appellarunt." *

'Go,† hide thyself in Italy: there will I make of thee a mighty people,' was, then, the voice of Heaven; and Æneas the Idumean, his aged father, and a few followers, pass to the coast of the Great Sea: they take ship at Joppa;‡ and, in a single vessel, along the shores of Africa they bend their course.

Virgil had, perhaps, some authority for making the Tyrian Dido contemporary with Æneas; and it is possible that these fugitive Edomites may have been saved from shipwreck, and hospitably entertained by this great queen. Her amour with Æneas may well be treated as the mere invention of the poet; particularly as history has assigned another and a nobler cause for Dido's death by her own hand. It is said, indeed, that the foundation of Carthage did not precede that of Rome by more than seventy years; but this is quite consistent with the account which makes Queen Dido the builder of a much older place,

* Aur. Victor, p. 18, (Delph. edit.) † 1 Kin. xvii. 3.
‡ Jonah i. 3.

called BURSA. But, however the fact may be, the argument we have in hand will be greatly assisted and supported by an examination and analysis of the proper-names found in the history of the earliest Carthaginians, as commonly related; and (assuming, for the present, that the PUNIC VERSES OF PLAUTUS contain a language identical almost with the Hebrew of the Kings of Israel), we shall have little difficulty in determining the derivation of these names. DIDO, or DIDON, (דִּידֹה, or דִּידֹן), then, is deducible from the root דּוּד, and will signify BELOVED-ONE; ELISSA,* is a compound of אֵל־אִשָּׁה, EL-ISHSHA, HERO-WOMAN, HERO-INE; ANNA, is the Hebrew KHANNAH,† MERCY; BURSA, is a contraction of בִּירָה־אִשָּׁה, BIRA-ISHSHA, BIRISSA, BIRSA, WOMAN'S-CITADEL; and CARTHAGE of קֶרֶת־הַגּוֹא, KERETH-HAGGO, KARTHHAGGO, KART-HAGO, CENTRAL (OR MIDDLEMOST) CITY. Following the history of the Carthaginians to the times of Hannibal, we may say that the name of Rome's great enemy contains the cry uttered by the priests of Baal, in the presence of Elijah and the Israelites, at Carmel: עֲנֵה־בַּעַל, ANNE-BAAL, ANNIBAL, O-BAAL-ANSWER. The appella-

* Rule Seven, p. 70. † Rule Eight, p. 70.

tion would seem to refer us to the famous oath. HAMILCAR is a compound of הַמֶּלֶךְ־כַּר, HAMMELEKCAR, HAMMILCAR, PASTURE-(or, COUNTRY)-KING, equivalent, perhaps, to the Latin REGULUS.

Sailing from Carthage, Æneas and his companions at length attain the country given to them by the prophecy of Isaac; and thereupon (in token that they hail it as their appointed rest), they burn their ship.* They obtain a grant of land from some petty king of the aborigines, whereon they build a little town, and (repeating the cry with which they touched the shore) they name it תְּרוֹ־יָהּ, TERO-JAH, TROJAH, TROJA,† SHOUT-(TO)-JEHOVAH. They call themselves LATINIM, and the country they inhabit לַטְיוֹן, LATJON, LATLAND, DWELLING-PLACE-OF-THE-LAT. The name LATINIM is deducible from לוּט, TO VEIL, TO HIDE: if we derive the word from the participle present of this verb, it will signify HIDING-ONES; if from the past participle (with a formative kamets ‡), it means HIDDEN-ONES. The singular of this word is לָטֵנִי, LATENI, LATINI,

* Dion. i. c. 72. † Serv. Æ. i. 6; vii. 158. Liv. i. c. 1.
‡ Rule Two, p. 65.

the syllable נִי, NI, (a portion of the pronoun אֲנִי, ANI, I), being postfixed to it. In the Biblical Hebrew the possessive case (if it may so be called), of this pronoun is formed by suffixing to the noun the letter I, and its objective by postfixing to the verb the syllable NI, preceded by the vowel-of-junction, or punctum-glutationis; which last may be A, E, or I. Thus, from EDOM the Hebrews form the nomen gentile EDOM-I, (OF-EDOM-I), AN EDOMITE. But this rule is not always observed; for, in the formation of the proper-names, we find the letter YOD used to denote both the possessive and objective forms of ANI. So SALATHIEL* is שְׁלָחֵנִי־אֵל.† With the Latins, however, the syllable NI appears most frequently as a suffix in the formation of the name: and from LAT they form LATINI, A LATIN; from TROJA, TROJANI, A TROJAN.

That these fugitive Idumeans designated themselves HIDERS, or HIDDEN-ONES, by Divine command, appears to be distinctly asserted by themselves, and, considered as imposed upon them by God's direction, the name (like many of the Hebrew proper-names) becomes prophetic; and describes a

* Page 62. † Psa. lxx. 1.

people whose origin (at the first well known), would become veiled and hidden, to all except the prophets of the Lord. The universal opinion of the ancients traces the name LATIUM to the act of hiding: it was, they say, the LURKING-PLACE of SATURN, callĕd by some a god, by others, an ancient monarch of the country. That the last tradition is the true one, and that Saturn is the good king Æneas, may be evidenced by the name itself. It appears to occur in two forms: סָתוּר־אֲנִי, SATUR-ANI, SATURNI, SATURN, HIDDEN-(AM)-I; and סָתוּר־אֲנִי־יָהּ, SATUR-ANI-IA, SATURNIA, HIDDEN-(AM)-I-(BY)-JEHOVAH. SATURN is to be considered as an abbreviation of SATURNIA, just as Josephus * should seem to call him BARUCH, (emphatically) BLESSED, whom our Lord speaks of † by his full name, BARACHIAS, JEHOVAH-HATH-BLESSED-(ME). "King Saturn," writes Justin,‡ "is said to have been of so much mildness, that under him neither was any one a slave, nor had private property any existence: but all things were enjoyed by all men in common, and without distinction; even as a patri-

* Bell. Jud. lib. iv. cap. v. 4.

† Matt. xxiii. 35.

‡ Lib. xliii. cap. 1.

mony belonging to them all." We have here a crowned Job. The name SATURNIA expounds the appellation LATINIM, and shews it to mean HIDDEN-ONES.

We have next to consider Æneas and his Idumeans as WORSHIPPERS OF JUPITER. The words of God to Moses, "THIS is my name, and this is my memorial, to all generations," might seem to contain a command that nothing should be added to the appellation JEHOVAH, nor anything diminished from it. The sequel of the history of the Exodus, however, proves that this is not the meaning of the text: "Fear ye not," said Moses to the people; "stand still, and see the salvation of Jehovah: JEHOVAH WILL FIGHT for you." "Then sang Moses and the children of Israel to Jehovah, saying, JEHOVAH IS A MAN OF WAR;" and hence, I apprehend, arose the compellation JEHOVAH-SABAOTH, JEHOVAH-OF-HOSTS, given by the Israelites to, and accepted of them by God, in memory of the destruction of Pharoah and his host. It is a condensation of the words JEHOVAH IS A MAN OF WAR. Now, the peculiar relation in which the Almighty stood to the Latins was that of a deliverer from bondage; death or bands being the alternatives offered by King David to the Edomites. They could not sing to Jehovah because He had triumphed gloriously, because His right hand had dashed in pieces the enemy; but they could say* to the Almighty, "We are indeed thy servants, O JEHOVAH; Thou hast LOOSED OUR BONDS: we will offer Thee the sacrifice of thanksgiving, and will call upon the name of Jehovah." Therefore, they endeavour to perpetuate the remembrance of the Divine mercy by the appellation יְהוֹ־פִּטֵּר, JEHO-PITTER, JOPITTER, JEHOVAH-(THAT)-HATH-SET-FREE, JEHOVAH-THE-ENFRANCHISER. The particulars of the worship offered to Jehovah by the patriarchs are easily discoverable in the history of these Latins. Clean beasts only could be laid upon His altar, which, from the name, אֵל־טוּר, EL-TUR, ALTAR,† GOD'S-ROCK, appears to have been formed of unhewn stones.‡ The victim was consumed by fire, whence the term, אוּרָה, URA, אָרָה, ARA, THE-BURNER. And the altar was placed before an OAK, thus rendered sacred.§ As with the patri-

* Psa. cxvi. 16. † Second Rule, p. 65. ‡ Deut. xxvii. 5.

§ Deut. xiii. 18; xviii. 1 (Sept. Trans.). Josh. xxiv. 26. Isa. i. 29. Liv. i. 10.

archs,* so with the oldest Latins, there was no distinct priesthood: no traces of the worship of any false deity are discoverable in their history; and when their descendants forgat God their Saviour, and were given up to strange delusions, to believe a lie, and to the worship of all the abominations of the heathen, the supremacy of Jupiter (degraded from the Creator of all things, into the son of his own creature,† Saturn or Æneas) was yet admitted and acknowledged. "Magnis de rebus dicere exordiens, a JOVE incipiendum: quem unum omnium deorum et hominum regem esse, omnes, indocti doctique, consentiunt," writes Cicero.‡

In connexion with the worship of JUPITER, we may consider the SATURNALIA in the light of the greatest solemnity of the oldest Latins; instituted (as its name and its observances testify), by ÆNEAS, SATURNI, or the HIDDEN-ONE, in honour of the Almighty, JEHOVAH-THE-ENFRANCHISER, the God who had delivered the Latins from the bonds prepared for them in Edom. The name of this festival in Phœnician is סָטוּרְנִי־אֵל־יָה, SATURNI-EL-IA, סָטֻרְנִילְיָה, SATURNILIA; and as

* Gen. xiv. 18. † Rom. i. 25.

‡ De Re. Pub. i. 37, (edit. Heinrich).

a noun, סָטְרְנַלְיָהּ, SATURNAL-IA, SATURNALIA, SATURNI-(or SATURN)-TO-JEHOVAH. The appellation is compounded of the names of the Deity in whose honour the festival was instituted, and of Æneas, by whom the observance of it was enjoined. The Saturnalia were instituted, say certain of the Romans, long before the foundation of Rome, in commemoration of the freedom and equality which prevailed on earth in the golden reign of Saturn; whilst others assert, that Janus first instituted the festival, in gratitude to Saturn, from whom he had learned agriculture. We shall see, hereafter, that Saturn and JANUS are the same person; JANUS being the DEIFIED SATURNI, or ÆNEAS. The celebration, we are told, was remarkable for the liberty which universally prevailed. In after-times, slaves (in the days of Saturn, servants), were allowed to speak with freedom upon every subject; friends made presents one to another; all animosity ceased; no criminals were executed; schools were shut; war was never declared; but all was mirth, and (with the Romans only) riot, and debauchery. The observance of the feast in the days of Æneas was, doubtless, in the spirit of that piety which called it into being; it answered to the Passover of the Jews, when divested of the prophetic character; and by it the Latins would make confession that, but for the mighty hand of JEHOVAH* their God, bringing them out of Edom, they had been servants in the land of their nativity. There were, of course, various other occasions on which the people came together to worship, and to make merry before the Lord; and these, as well as the Saturnalia, and others having distinguishing names, appear to have been comprehended under the general term CONSUALIA, כְּנֶס־הוּא־אֶלְיָה, CONES - HU - EL - IA, כְּנֶסוּאֶלְיָה, CONSUELIA; as a noun, CONSUALIA, A-GATHERING-(IS)-IT-TO-JEHOVAH. Thus, the festival celebrated by Romulus when the Sabine virgins were carried off, is said by some† to have been held in honour of CONSUS, by others of NEPTUNUS. The last word seems to be the Phœnician נְפְתֻהוּן, NE-PETHE-UN, NEPTUN, A DILATING (or EXPANDING), to wit, of the heart; a day of feasting and joy; of sending portions one to another, and gifts to the poor.‡ It was, probably, the feast of the SATURNALIA, or

* Deut. v. 15.

† Liv. i. cap. 9. Cic. De R. P. i. p. 56. Dion. ii. c. 30, 31. Plut. Rom. xiv.

‡ Esth. ix. 22.

PALILIA. In later times, the Romans appear to have added the termination ALIA to the names of various festivals (as, for instance, the MATRALIA, clearly of foreign origin), without having the slightest suspicion of its true and primitive meaning.

* * * *

TROY being built, and the worship of God established, the names of the different people by whom Æneas and his Edomites were surrounded fall next under our consideration: and these, I should say, were comprehended by these Idumeans under two grand divisions, the SABINES, and the ETRUSCANS; the first appellation including all but the Tuscans. SABINI, SABINIM, סבני, סבנים from סבב SABAB, TO SURROUND, would mean NEIGHBOURS; and portions of these SABINES would, in process of time, receive distinctive appellations: as, שָׁמֵן־אִישׁ, SHAMEN-ISH, SHAMNIS, SAMNIS, ROBUST-MAN, SAMNITE; שֹׁבְלִים, SOBELIM, שָׁבְלִים, SABELLIM, POURERS-OVER, SABELLIANS, the people who afterwards overran so large part of Italy. It is manifest that the Roman story contradicts itself in making Titus Tatius the king of a whole nation;

he could be no more than the ruler of some small Sabine town and state, little, if anything, superior to the Rome of Romulus in power and importance. With regard to the ETRUSCANS, till some better origin than that assigned them by Herodotus shall be discovered, we must be content to call them Mæonians, deriving their Grecian appellation, TYRRHENIANS, from the Tyrrhenus who led them into Italy, and speaking a tongue Greek in its original, but completely corrupted, and almost swallowed up in the language of the Umbrians, amongst whom they dwelt. The name TUSCAN would seem to be of Phœnician origin, and would, therefore, have been given to them by the Latins. טוּר־אִישׁ, TUR-ISH, TURISK,* TURSK, (whence the corruptions TURSICI, TUSCI, ETRUSCI), WALL-MAN; an appellation well descriptive of a people dwelling in towers, castles, and walled cities, and as opposed to the SABINIM, who lived in villages and towns destitute of walls.† And may not the name RASENA, given to this people (in a single passage only) by Dionysius, be Phœnician also; and, like the PERSA of the Latins, referrible to their horsemanship? "Persis," writes Bochart,‡ "nomen

* Rule Eight, p. 70. † Plut. Rom. 16. ‡ Phalg. iv. 10.

fuit ab equitatu, quo maxime valebant; equitare a teneris edocti." According to this derivation, PERSA, PERSIAN, will be of Phœnician origin; פָּרָשָׁה, PARASA, פְּרָשָׁה, PERASA, פְּרְשָׁה, PERSA, HORSEMAN: and so from רֶסֶן, RESEN, A BRIDLE, may come רְסוּנָה, רְסֶנָה, RASENA, A-BRIDLER, A-MAN-OF-THE-BRIDLE. Horses and horsemen, chariots and charioteers, fill a large space in the pictorial representations found on the vases and other monuments of Etruscan antiquity which have been preserved to us; and, according to Livy,* (perhaps, also, Tacitus,†) the Romans borrowed their horse-races from this very people. Even the name *Τυρρηνος* may be only another form of TURISH: טוּר־אֱנוֹשׁ, TURENOS, WALL-MAN.

* * * *

ÆNEAS, we are told, obtained in marriage the daughter of the king by whom, on his arrival in Italy, he had been hospitably received and entertained. A similar honour subsequently attended another flying Edomite. "When David was in Edom,‡ Hadad fled, he and certain of his father's servants with him, to go into Egypt: and they came

* Lib. i. c. 35. † Annal. xiv. 21.

‡ 1 Kings xi. 17.

H

to Pharaoh king of Egypt, who gave him an house, and appointed him victuals, and gave him land: and Hadad found great favour in the sight of Pharaoh, so that he gave him to wife the sister of his own wife." This Hadad was 'of the king's seed in Edom;' and the Roman story makes Æneas, also, of royal extraction. The name LAVINIA must, being Phœnician, have been given by Æneas to his wife: לוה־אני־יה, LAVA-ANI-IA, LAVINI-IA, LAVINIA, JEHOVAH-HATH-ADHERED-TO-ME. "Jehovah is on my side," says David; "I will not fear what man doeth unto me." Livy adds, that this event confirmed the hope of the new-comers that their wanderings would terminate in a permanent settlement in the land, a persuasion which seems to find expression in the name imposed by Æneas on the first child of the marriage: אֶשְׁכֹּן־אֲנִי, ASACCENANI, ASCCENNI, ASCANI,* I-SHALL-DWELL-PEACEABLY. According to Dionysius, the first Silvius of the story was also the son of Æneas and Lavinia: שְׁלִוִי· שָׁלֵו, SILVI, PEACEFUL-AND-PROSPEROUS-(AM)-I. Another town is built, called LAVINIUM; but whether in honour of this Lavinia or not may be doubted:

* Second Rule, p. 65.

for the name LAVINIM, ADHERENTS, in the mouths of these godly or (so Dionysius calls them) 'god-like' men, would be equivalent to the term BRETHREN as used by the Christians of the Apostolic age; and thus LAVINION would receive its name, directly, from the LAVINES, as its builders.

And here the mortal acts of Æneas, so far as they affect the proper-names recorded by the story, appear to have their end. With his wars, the present argument, which confines itself to an examination of the legend as exhibited in these names, has no concern. If Æneas warred, we may well believe that he waged it in the spirit of Abraham, when he smote the kings, and brought again his brother Lot, and his goods, and the women also, and the people; and of Job, when he brake the jaws of the wicked, and plucked the spoil out of his teeth. He was buried, writes Livy, on the banks of the river Numicius; but, according to Dionysius, no man knew either the place of his sepulchre or the manner of his death; and by many he was supposed to have been translated to heaven without tasting death. After his removal from this earth he was called JUPITER INDIGES; and in the JANUS, יָהּ־נוֹ, JAH-NU,

JANU, OUR-JEHOVAH, of the Roman story, we seem to recognize the DEIFIED ÆNEAS, one of the DÆMONS, or DII MINORES, of the Latins. The appellation OUR-JEHOVAH is a bold, and (to us) irreverent expression; a character which, but that they occur in Scripture, we should, perhaps, attach to the words, "He calleth them gods unto whom the word of God came."* The term OUR may, however, so restrict and qualify the name as to render it equivalent to A-GOD-UPON-EARTH, or, A-GUARDIAN-ANGEL. The Rabbins derive the Hebrew SHADDAI, THE ALMIGHTY, from אֲשֶׁר־דַּי, ASHER-DAI, WHO-(IS)-SUFFICIENCY; and the Latin DEUS may have the like origin: דַּי־הוּא, DAI-HU, דֵּי־הוּא, DE-HU, DEU, SUFFICIENCY-(IS)-HE. Now the word DÆMON (of which DEUS MINOR appears to be a later, and exact, translation) would be formed from the pluralis excellentiæ דַּיִּים, DAIM, with the diminutive וֹן, ON, DAIMON, DEMON; and, according to this derivation, it would signify A MINOR GOD, A MINOR SUFFICIENCY. "Deus," says Festus, "dictus est, quod ei nihil desit." And so ENOCH and ELIJAH, translated to heaven, and

* John x. 35.

made equal with the angels, and partakers of the Divine nature, became SUFFICIENCIES: but, forasmuch as their sufficiency was of God * alone, these Edomites seem to have denominated them (in common with the angels) DÆMONES, DII MINORES, MINOR GODS, MINOR SUFFICIENCIES. That the oldest Latins offered to Æneas, or their other dæmons, anything approaching to divine worship, there should seem to be no proof: in all probability they thought and spoke of them as the Jews do of their own Elijah; as of one who, though exalted to the highest heaven, is yet cognizant of the doings, and greatly interested in the welfare of his brethren upon earth. The SEMO SANCUS of the Latins appears to be the JUPITER INDIGES, or JANUS, in another form. For, if we read the Hebrew שָׁנָה, SHANAH, with the hardened H,† or KH, then שְׁמוֹ־שָׁנְחוּ, SHEMO SHANĔKHU, SEMO SANCU, will signify HIS-NAME-HAVE-THEY-CHANGED, THE-DEITY-OF-THE-CHANGED-NAME.

Other circumstances indicating the identity of Æneas with Saturn, and of Saturn with Janus, may be detected amidst the corruptions and distortions

* 2 Cor. iii. 5.

† Rule Eight, p. 71.

of the true legend. Thus, Saturn is driven to Italy by the arms of Jupiter,* in the language of Scripture, by the sword of Jehovah and of David; Janus receives the fugitive Saturn, and makes him a sharer of his throne;† Janus coins money, one side of which he impresses with his own effigy, and the other with a representation of the ship which brought Saturn into Italy; and this ship appears also on the reverse of the Roman AS, which, from the earliest times, had on it the double-headed Janus.

* * * *

We may now proceed with the examination and analysis of the proper-names connected with the legendary history of Rome, in the order in which they are presented to us by the books of Livy.

Ascanius,‡ the son and successor of Æneas, built for himself a new town, called ALBA LONGA. "He transferred," writes Dionysius,§ "both the inhabitants of Lavinium and the other Latins, who were desirous of a better habitation, to his new-built city." The name ALBA LONGA, treated as belonging to the Latin of Livy, and translated into

* Ovid, Fast. lib. i. v. 235.

† Macrob. Saturnal. lib. i. c. 7.

‡ Liv. lib. i. cap. 3.

§ Lib. i. cap. 56.

our own tongue, would be equivalent to LONG WHITE-TOWN. The appellation ALBA is referred by the ancients to the omen of the WHITE SOW,* already noticed; but, if this animal were, in reality, the star which led Æneas into Italy, or if, as Lycophron has it, the sow was black, some other reason for the name ALBA must be discoverable. The city, according to Livy, was called LONGA from its situation, being extended on the ridge of a hill. With the assistance of Strabo, we shall be able to refer the words ALBA LONGA to the Phœnician, the language of Æneas and his followers. ALBA was seated in the middle of the dominions of its founder,† and it was the political centre of the Latin confederacy. Now, the 'middle,' or 'centre,' of anything, is in Hebrew called its 'heart;' as, for example, the 'heart of the sea,' the 'heart of heaven.' "The depths were congealed in the heart of the sea."‡ "And the mountain burned with fire unto the midst (literally, the heart) of heaven."§ Cities, with the Hebrews, are of the feminine gender, and so הַלִּבָּה, HALLĬBA, HALLBA,‖ ALBA, THE HEART, would be

* Serv. on Æn. i. v. 270. † Strabo, lib. v. ‡ Exod. xv. 8.
§ Deut. iv. 11. ‖ Ninth Rule, p. 71.

one name of the city built by Ascanius, expressive both of its locality, as placed in the centre of his kingdom, and of its political position, as the leader of the confederated Latins. In Second Samuel * we find a place called LO-DEBAR,† WITHOUT-PESTILENCE; so named, no doubt, from its salubrity; and if to the particle LO, WITHOUT, we subjoin a word of similar meaning with DEBAR, we obtain the appellation לֹא־נֶגַע, LO-NĔGA, LONGA, WITHOUT PLAGUE; and ALBA LONGA, the city of Ascanius, is in reality ALBA WITHOUT-PLAGUE, ALBA THE SALUBRIOUS. And such has been the character of the Alban Mount, and the adjacent country, even to the present day.

The transference of the supreme government of the Latins to the city of the Mons Albanus carried with it the great altar of the Latin Jupiter; thenceforward called לָטִי־הַר, LATI-HAR, JUPITER LATIAR, JUPITER OF THE LATIAN MOUNT.

On the death of Ascanius, Sylvius, his son, (according to Dionysius, his brother), ascended the throne. He was, says Livy (innocently enough),

* Chap. xvii. 27. † Second Rule, p. 5.

"casu quodam in silvis natus."* This Sylvius was the father of Æneas Silvius, who begot Latinus Sylvius; and with Latinus Sylvius originated certain colonies called by the historian PRISCI LATINI. The translation of these terms by the words ANCIENT LATINS is contradictory of the story; since both Lavinium and Alba itself would have a prior and preferable title to the name. "PRISCUS," writes Niebuhr, "was certainly the title of a people; and has exactly the same form and character with the national names, Tuscus, Cascus, and Opscus;" and this historian treats the appellation as equivalent to PRISCI ET LATINI. But to this word, also, a Phœnician derivation, perfectly consistent with the origin of these colonies, may be assigned. For, if from the Hebrew PARASH, TO SEPARATE, we form the participial noun פְּרִישׁ, PĔRISH, and (Rule Eight †) pronounce this word with the hardened H, PĔRISKIM LATINIM, PRISKIM LATINIM, PRISCI LATINI, will mean SEPARATED LATINS; colonies separated, as it were, from the womb of Alba, their common mother. Livy does not call the earliest inhabitants of Rome 'Prisci Romani,' but 'Veteres Romani;'‡

* Lib. i. cap. 3. † Page 71. ‡ Lib. i. cap. 33.

and the term PRISCUS, in the sense of separated, is, when applied to the first Tarquin, in entire accordance with his story. For the name TARQUINIUS PRISCUS would be then of Latin origin, assumed by this king on becoming a citizen of Rome; and it would signify TARQUINIAN SEPARATIST, SECEDER FROM TARQUINII. And Dionysius furnishes us with the reason why Lavinium was reckoned amongst these Prisci Latini. It was, he says,* re-peopled by the Albans, who sent back some of their own people from Alba to Lavinium, to live there.

* * * *

Little can be made of the names of the kings from Sylvius to Romulus and Remus: the list, as Niebuhr asserts of it, seems to be a very late and clumsy fabrication. To one of them, however, Romulus Sylvius, a Phœnician origin may be attributed. רוֹם־מוּל־הוּא, ROM-MUL-HU, ROMULU, BE-RISEN-BEFORE-HIM, STAND-UP-BEFORE-HIM. "Thou shalt rise up before the hoary head, and honour the face of the old man;"† and the veneration in which Job was held by his countrymen is asserted in the text, "The young men

* Lib. i. cap. 67. † Lev. xix. 32.

saw me, and hid themselves: even the aged arose, and stood up."* Romulus Sylvius, thus translated, will therefore be SYLVIUS THE VENERATED. This name, however, though consisting of the same letters, is not, I imagine, identical with that of the founder of Rome. The last contains a word of very different signification.

* * * *

We have next to read the legend of Romulus and Remus in connection with the proper-names to which it has given birth; and from these names to discover how much of the tale belongs to the genuine and ancient tradition of the Romans. The story of RHEA SILVIA (רִיאָה), LOOKED-AT SILVIA, SIGHTLY SILVIA, appears to involve the expression of the vow attributed by the Scriptures to Jephthah the Gileadite. He, we are told, vowed a vow, by virtue of which his only daughter became the Lord's, and was devoted to perpetual virginity; employed (as it should seem), in the services of the tabernacle of God. "He did with her according to his vow which he had vowed, and she knew no man." And the irrevocable vow, the vow from which Jephthah could not 'go back,' was

* Job xxix. 8.

made by the words, "I will offer her up for a (WHOLE)-BURNT-OFFERING." Not that this daughter of Israel was to be put to death; for the service was to be a reasonable service, the sacrifice a living sacrifice, holy, and acceptable to God: but (as the Jews rightly understand the nature of the vow), she was, symbolically, to be made a holocaust, the flesh whereof was wholly the Lord's, and no part of it could be reserved by the worshipper for himself. So Amulius causes Rhea Silvia to become A VESTAL; and, as a consequence, the obligation of perpetual chastity is laid upon her: she is made אִשָּׁה־עַל־אֵשׁ, ISHSHA-AL-ESH, אֵשֶׁת־עַל־אִשׁ, ESHETH-AL-ISH, אֶשְׁתָּלֵשׁ, ESTALIS * (in later Latin, and with the V prefixed by the Romans to many words derived to them from the Greeks), VESTALIS; A-WOMAN-(LAID)-UPON-THE-FIRE, (symbolically), A-FEMALE-BURNT-SACRIFICE. The Romans, in the times of their subsequent ignorance of God and of His service, found in this name the goddess VESTA, and her sacred fire: but as we discover no traces, prior to the days of Numa, of any worship amongst the Latins save that offered by them to their Jupiter,

* Rule Seven, p. 70.

this holy flame would be the fire of His altar, which, like that of the altar of burnt-offerings * in the tabernacle of the Jews, might be kept always burning, and be never suffered to go out. The author of Judges adds to his narrative, "And it was a custom in Israel;" which words seem to have been misunderstood by the commentators, and they refer (I apprehend) to the vow of Jephthah and its consequences, not to the succeeding verse, and the yearly lamentations of the daughters of Israel for Jephthah's daughter. Now it is quite possible that the Latins, as descendants of Esau, might possess many customs and observances found also amongst the sons of Jacob, and deriving their existence from times more ancient than the other institutions of the Mosaic Dispensation; and the vow here recorded may have been one of them; a portion, perhaps, of the rites of the patriarchal religion, even as it existed in the days of Noah and his sons. It is certain that the law of the Levirate Nuptials was obligatory on the descendants of Abraham centuries before the Exodus of the Israelites from Egypt.†

The examination and analysis of the names attaching to the story of the exposure and preserva-

* Lev. vi. 13. † Gen. xxxviii. 8.

tion of the twin brothers must be preceded by extracting from the writings of Dionysius the tale, as he had it * from the lost history of Fabius Pictor. "By the order of Amulius, some of the king's officers took the children in a cradle (or trough, σκαφη), and carried them to the river, designing to throw them into it. When they drew near, and perceived that the Tiber, swelled by continual rains, had exceeded its natural bed, and had overflowed the plains, they came down from the top of the Palatine Hill to that part of the water which lay nearest, (for they could advance no farther), and set down the cradle upon the flood, where it washed the foot of the hill. The cradle floated for some time: then, as the waters retired by degrees from the utmost verge, striking against a stone, it overturned and threw out the children, who lay crying and wallowing in the mud. Upon this, a she-wolf, that had just whelped, appeared; and, her teats being distended with milk, gave them her paps to suck, and with her tongue licked off the mud with which they were besmeared. In the meantime, some shepherds happened to be driving their flocks to pasture (for the place was now become passable),

* Diony. lib. i. cap. 79.

and one of them, SEEING THE WOLF THUS CHERISHING THE CHILDREN, was, for some time, struck dumb with astonishment and disbelief of what he saw: then, going away, and GETTING TOGETHER AS MANY OF THE SHEPHERDS AS HE COULD, he carried them to see the sight themselves. When THESE, ALSO, drew near, and saw the wolf cherishing the children AS IF THEY HAD BEEN HER YOUNG-ONES, and the children HANGING ON HER AS ON THEIR MOTHER, they imagined they saw SOMETHING SUPERNATURAL, and advanced together, hallooing, to terrify the creature. The wolf, not much frightened at the approach of the men, but as if she had been tame, gently withdrew from the children, GREATLY DESPISING the mob of shepherds. There was, not far off, a holy place, covered with a thick wood, and a hollow rock. When the wolf came to this place, she hid herself. The grove is no longer in existence, but the cave is contiguous to the Palatine buildings, and is to be seen in the way that leads to the Circus; and near it stands a temple in which a statue is placed representing this incident: it is A WOLF SUCKLING TWO CHILDREN: they are in brass, and are of ancient workmanship. As soon as the wolf was gone, the shepherds took up the children, and were very desirous to bring them up; and an overseer of the king's swineherds, whose name was Faustulus, a man of humanity, having received them by general consent, carried them home to his wife. As they grew up, he gave one the name of ROMULUS, the other, that of REMUS. The life of the children was that of HERDSMEN. They lived by their own labour, and, generally, on the mountains, in cottages of one story, which they built with wood and reeds; of which, one, called THE COTTAGE OF ROMULUS, remains even to this day, in the corner as you turn from the Palatine Hill to the Circus. It is kept sacred by those to whom the care of it is committed, who add to it no ornaments to render it more venerable; but, if any part of it is injured, whether by tempest or lapse of time, they repair the damage, and are careful to restore it, as nearly as may be, to its former condition."

Now, whilst the existence of the brazen wolf, and the cottage of Romulus, attest the popular belief of the legend, as related by Fabius Pictor, so will the names attributed by the Romans to the chief actors in the story carry it upwards to times more ancient than the oldest of their historians, and to the reach of testimony deriveable from a language, the existence of which, as a component portion of his mother-tongue, would never be suspected by any Roman wishing to corrupt the tradition of the fathers of the city, or to produce a tale till then unheard. Here, first, we meet with LUPERCA, a goddess who caused the she-wolf to treat Romulus and Remus so kindly; and thus named, say some, from LUPA and PARCO. By the Hebrews the wolf was called ZEEB, and by the Greeks LUKOS: LUP therefore would be the domestic name of the animal, its appellative amongst the aborigines of Latium. If, then, to LUP we subjoin the feminine of the Hebrew פֹּרֵק, A SNATCHER-AWAY, A DELIVERER,* we form the name LUP-פֹּרְקָה, LUPPIRKA, THE-WOLF-THE-SHE-DELIVERER. Next, we have another goddess, RUMINA, who presided over infants whilst at the breast, and the FIG-TREE, called FICUS RUMINALIS, under which the suckling of Romulus and Remus by the she-wolf is supposed to have taken place.† In the Hebrew,

* Lam. v. 8.

† Liv. lib. i. cap. 4.

רעה אמנה ,רע־אמנה, RO-OMENA ,רומנה, RUMENA, will signify SHEPHERD-NOURISHER; and, if to this word we add the Latin formative ALIS, FICUS RUMINALIS will be the FIG-TREE OF THE-SHEPHERD-SUCKLER (or NOURISHER): but if we take the termination ALIS to be Hebrew, and to represent the words על (AL) and איש (ISH), then the whole name רומנה־על־איש, רומינליש, RUMINALIS, added to FICUS, will give the appellation THE FIG-TREE OF THE-SHEPHERD-SUCKLER-IN-THE-SIGHT-OF-MAN. And the suckled shepherd must be the LUPERCUS of the Romans, Rome's founder Romulus, before the building of the city, and by his foster-father called LUP-פרק, LUP-PĔRĔC, LUPERC, WOLF-DELIVERED; and the LUPERCALIA, LUPERC-אל־יה, LUPERC-TO-JEHOVAH; a feast of praise and thanksgiving dedicated by the shepherd king to God, in memory of his preservation by the she-wolf. In a preceding page, I have resolved the appellation ROMULU into the Hebrew רום־מול־הוא, ROM-MUL-HU, with the signification VENERATED; but this name, though it might have been given by the Roman people to their king, could never have originated with Faustulus, or been borne by Romulus during his shepherd life. A very different derivation may, perhaps, be assigned to the title of Rome's first king; and it may be treated as a compound of the words רֹעֶה מוּל, רֹעֶ־מוּל, ROMUL, or, with the emphatic הוּא, ROMULU; A-SHEPHERD-HERETOFORE, THE-QUONDAM-SHEPHERD. On the last supposition, the appellation must have been assumed by the king himself, who, like God's servant David, had been taken from the sheepfolds and from following the ewes great with young; and it will bear testimony both to the humility and magnanimity of its royal author, and to the certainty of the legend of the she-wolf. The grand objection to this derivation of the name arises from the fact, that in the small store of Hebrew we possess, MUL, (ANTE), is never used in respect of time, but has reference to place only. On the other hand, we have the word ETHMUL, with the signification HERETOFORE, and this would appear to be a compound of MUL and the particle ETH (אֶת־מוּל); whence, perhaps, arises a strong presumption that MUL itself, divested of this prefix, might also possess the meaning belonging to the compound word. In either case, ROMULUS must, before the building of the city, have had some other designation; and his first name will, I imagine, be found in the appellation LUPERC. This name appears also in the word LUPERCAL, (Luperc-עָל), LUPERC'S-HEIGHT, designating either the whole Mons Palatinus, or that portion of it where the she-wolf came to the rescue of the sons of Rhea Silvia. REM, or REMU, (רְאֵם, or רֵאמדוּא), signifies in Hebrew, WILD-BULL, BUFFALO, an animal still inhabiting the country between Rome and Ostia.* The depths of the religious ignorance into which the once wise and understanding Romans fell may be estimated and evidenced by the treatment which the story of Romulus and Remus met with at their hands in after-times. For, from this source alone, they seem to have derived their divinities VESTA, LUPERCA, RUMINA, and LUPERCUS; all of whom appear to be mere creations of philological speculation, employed in determining the derivations of the words VESTALIS, LUPERCAL, RUMINALIS, and LUPERCALIA. They became vain in their imaginations, and their foolish heart was darkened; they forgot the name of the God of Æneas; they lifted up their hands to strange gods; they provoked Jehovah to anger with their inven-

* Rome in the Nineteenth Century. Edin. 1820. Vol. iii. 413.

tions; and the plague of their perverted theology brake in upon them.

* * * *

ROMA. The name of the Eternal City, רוֹמָה, ROMAH, is pure Hebrew; a noun formed from רוּמָה, RUMAH, the feminine of the past participle of the verb רוּם, RUM, by the change of SHUREK (U) into KHOLEM (O); and it signifies THAT-HAS-BEEN-EXALTED. The use of the past participle in the formation of the word appears to express, not merely the position of the URBS SEPTICOLLIS, but the persuasion of the founders of this DOMINA GENTIUM, that (in the words of Obadiah *), their city would "exalt herself as the eagle, and set her nest amongst the stars."

POMŒRIUM. When referred to the Hebrew, may be treated as a compound of פּוֹ, PO, the enclitic מוֹ, MO, (after the form כְּמוֹ), עִיר, IR, and the formative יוֹן, ION: פּוֹמוֹ־עִיר־יוֹן, POMOIRION, POMŒRIUM, THE-HITHERTO-OF-THE-CITY.

REMURIA, רֵאמוּ־רִיָּאָה, REMU-RIA, will, in Hebrew, signify REMUS'-CHOICE; the hill, some miles below Rome, on the Tiber, where Remus wished the city to be built.

* Verse 4.

PALATIUM. The Hebrew פֶּלֶט, PALAT, ONE THAT ESCAPES, joined to the formative יוֹן, ION, will make the Mons Palatinus mean PLACE-OF-THE-PALAT, (OR REFUGEE). The hill would therefore be so called as the REFUGIUM and dwelling-place of Romulus and Remus, delivered from Amulius by the she-wolf, and nurtured by the shepherds; and hence would come the tale that Romulus made Rome an asylum for runaway slaves. That such would be received and entertained by him we may believe, for so had the sons of Jacob been commanded; but it does not follow that Romulus resorted to this expedient to increase the population of his city. "Thou shalt not deliver unto his master the servant which is escaped from his master unto thee; he shall dwell with thee in that place which he shall choose, in one of thy gates, where it liketh him best." *

CAPITOLIUM. In Hebrew, כַּפִּי־תֹלִיוֹן, CAPPI-TOL-ION, CAPITOLION, THE-PLACE-(WHEREAT)-TO-UPLIFT-THE-HAND; the place of worship and prayer, and of the 'lifting up of holy hands.' † Here, according to Livy, stood the oak (and, no doubt, the altar) sacred to Jupiter; and

* Deut. xxiii. 15. † 1 Tim. ii. 8.

in this holy mount, thence also called צַר־פֶּה־יָהּ, TSAR-PE-IAH, TARPEIA, ROCK-OF-THE-MOUTH-OF-JEHOVAH, the devout Romans awaited God's answers to their prayers. With the Greeks and Romans, the Hebrew TSADDE, or TS, is represented by S, or T, or Z; but they seem to have been unable to enunciate this letter as pronounced by the Jews. Jerome, speaking of it, says, "Zadde, quam nostræ aures penitus reformidant."

COMITIUM. By the Romans of the Augustan age derived from CON and ITUM; but in the Hebrew קֹמֶט־יוֹן, KOMET-ION, COMITION, PLACE-OF-FETTERING, of TYING-HAND-AND-FOOT. Here the assembled people gave their assent to laws, and so put on themselves the shackles of legal obligation.

REX. This word, referred to the Hebrew, will be a compound of רָגַע, RAGA, TO STIR UP, AGITATE, PUT INTO COMMOTION, and אִישׁ, ISH, MAN; רָגַע־אִישׁ, רֶגִישׁ, REGIS, REGS, REX. The elective king of the Romans was the great STIMULATOR, PROVOCATOR, of their TUMULTUS, or LEVY EN MASSE.

TRIBUS. The word TĔRIB, by contraction

TRIB, considered as a derivative from רָבָה, RABAH, TO BE NUMEROUS, appears to be analogous with the Latin MULTITUDO, and the Greek ΠΛΗΘΟΣ; and to denote the aggregate of the individuals, whether Ramnes, Titienses, or Luceres, of which it was made up: תְּ־רִבָּה, תְּרִבִּים, TRIBBEH, TRIBBIM, TRIBE, TRIBES.

RAMNES. TITIENSES. LUCERES. The resolution of the names of the tribes into Hebrew, converts them from nations into three distinct castes, composed of the nobles, the husbandmen, and the handicraftsmen. The obsolete ENESH, from which the common Hebrew plural ANASHIM is formed, will (the authority of Festus admitted) be found in each of these appellations. Thus, רָם־אֱנָשׁ, RAM-ENES,* (by contraction) RAMNES,† is, literally, HIGH-FELLOW; and טִיט־אֱנָשׁ, TIT-ENES, TIT-ENS, or, with Yod inserted, TITIENS, means SOIL-MAN, MAN-OF-THE-SOIL, HUSBANDMAN. The Hebrew ICCAR, DIGGER, PLOUGHMAN, HUSBANDMAN, refers us to a root ACAR, synonymous (as in the Arabic) with כָּרָה, CARAH, TO DIG; and if to the participle of this verb we prefix the particle לֹא, LO, (or the Latin NON), and

* Rule Seven, p. 70. † Rule Nine, p. 71.

subjoin to it the word אִישׁ, ISH, MAN, we form the appellation לֹא־אִכֵּר־אִישׁ, LO-OCER-IS, LOOCERIS, LUCERIS, NON-DIGGING-MAN, HANDICRAFTSMAN. If, as Festus asserts, the members of the third tribe were also called LUCERENSES, the word ENES, as found in RAMNES and TITIENS, will enter into the composition of this name, and LUCER-ENES, LUCERENS, will be exactly equivalent to LUCERIS.

SENATOR. אֲשֶׁר־נָטוֹר, ASHER-NATOR, שֶׁנָּטוֹר, SHENATOR, SENATOR,* WHO-IS-TO-WATCH, WHO-IS-TO-GUARD; the senators being peculiarly those to whom, as to guardians and watchmen, the safety and welfare of the people were committed.

PATER. "Patres certe ab honore appellati," writes Livy; and his notion of the origin of this title, as borne by the Roman senators, may be correct, without giving the name the signification of 'father,' 'parent,' which, in the vocabulary of this historian, appears to be the Greek Πατηρ, and to be derived to the Latin directly from the language of the Greeks. The Hebrew פָּטֻר, PATER, signifies ONE WHO IS RELIEVED FROM SERVICE, as in

* Rule Seven, p. 70.

FIRST CHRONICLES:* "And these are the singers, chief of the fathers of the Levites, who, remaining in the chambers, were PATURIM, FREE FROM (all other) SERVICE; for they were employed in that work (or service) day and night." And so the ROMAN SENATOR, engaged at all times in the Senate-house in his capacity of watchman for the welfare, and guardian of the lives and liberty of the people, was a PATER, or Pater-אִישׁ, PATERIS, PATRIS; one relieved from the military and all other services incumbent on the residue of the members of the state.

PATRICIUS. PLEBS. PLEBS, or PLEBIS, will, in Hebrew, be a compound of פֶּה־לֵב־אִישׁ, PĔ-LĒB-IS, by contraction, PLEBIS, PLEBS, MOUTH-HEARTED-MAN, MOUTH-MINDED-MAN; one whose whole attention is taken up and engrossed by the care of providing for his daily subsistence. The name PATRIC, or PATRICI, should seem to be the opposite of PLEBS, and to be derived from the root TARAK, which occurs but once in the Hebrew of the Bible: פֶּה־טְרָכִי, PETEREKI, PATRIKI, A-FLINGER-AWAY-OF-THE-MOUTH; one relieved from the cares

* Chap. ix. 33.

incident to the task of making daily provision for his existence; one who, unlike the PLEBS, does not 'live from hand to mouth.'

PATRONUS. CLIENS. In many cases the Hebrew termination ON has the force of a diminutive; and so from ISH, A MAN, they denominate the pupilla of the eye ISHSHON AYIN, THE LITTLE MAN OF THE EYE. If, then, to the name PATER, considered as an appellative peculiar to the Senator of the Romans, we subjoin this formative ON, we obtain the name PATER-ON, by contraction PATRON, with the signification PATER MINOR, that is, MINOR SENATOR, MINOR WATCHMAN, MINOR GUARDIAN. And such was the relation in which the PATRONUS stood to his CLIENTS, as the guardian of their individual interests, and as contrasted with the SENATOR, to whose keeping the welfare of the whole body of the people was entrusted. The SENIORES and JUNIORES PATRUM are often placed in opposition by Livy; but (as Niebuhr remarks), in supposing all these PATRES to be senators, differing in temper according to their ages, both he and Dionysius must certainly have been mistaken. Thus, in Livy's narrative of the conduct of L. Furius and C. Manlius, when accused, we read that "circumeunt sordidati non Plebem magis quam juniores Patrum;"* they canvassed not merely the plebs, the populace, but such of the Patricians as had clients amongst the plebs; such of the Patricians as were also Patrons. For it is unnecessary to suppose that every PATRICIAN was also A PATRON: on the contrary, the privilege of receiving persons into clientship is said, in the first instance, to have been claimed by the Patricians of the Ramnes, to the exclusion of the Patricians belonging to the other tribes; and even amongst the Ramnes, there may have been Patricians without a single client.

CLIENS. חִלִּיתָ־אֱנֹשׁ, KILLE-ENES, KILLIENS, KLIENS, will, in Hebrew, denote A SUPPLICATOR OF ANOTHER, ONE WHO IMPLORES THE FAVOUR OF ANOTHER.

PALILIA. The foundation-day of Rome was celebrated on the twenty-first of April, being (it is said) the festival of PALES, the goddess of shepherds; but the term PALILIA, when referred to the Hebrew, discloses a very different signification. פִּלֵּא־אֱלֹיָהּ, PALA-EL-IAH, PALILIA, HE-HATH-DEDICATED - (THE CITY) - TO - JEHOVAH,

* Liv. lib. ii. cap. 54.

IT-IS-DEDICATED-TO-JEHOVAH. It should seem impossible to read the history of Romulus without perceiving that he acknowledged no god save the Jupiter of his fathers; and that Mars, Vesta, and the other divinities of the story, are the creations and fictions of the ignorance of later times. And may not this very name PALILIA have been the SECRET (or LESS KNOWN) NAME of Rome, perpaucis cognitum, neminique revelandum; and involving that of the Tutelaris Romæ Deus, by some believed to be Jupiter himself,* that is, IA?

QUIRIS. קִיר־אִישׁ, KIR-IS, CITY-MAN, CITIZEN, literally, WALL-MAN, one living within the walls of the city, as opposed to those who dwelt in the open country. The Roman Q is said by Quintilian to have been obtained from the Greeks, and to be the KOPPA of their alphabet; but both these letters will best be referred directly to the Phœnician KOPH.

TALASSIUS. TALASSIO. TALASSUS. THALASSIUS. Plutarch seems to have preserved the true origin of this cry; and the uplifting of the bride, by which it was accompanied, will enable us to trace it to a Phœnician origin. It was, he

* Macrob. Saturnal, iii. 5.

says, the signal given by Romulus * for the commencement of the rape; and it is worthy of observation that Plutarch derived this version of the word from a Carthaginian, Sextius Sylla, who, speaking the Phœnician tongue, would recognize in it a meaning lost to the Romans and the Greeks. This nuptial cry should seem, then, to be a corruption of תֹּל־אִשָּׁה, TOL-ISHSHA, תַּלִּשָּׁה, TALISHSHA, TALISSA, LIFT-WOMAN.

FERETRIUS. פָּרַע־אֶת־עִירִי, PARA-ETH-IRI, PHERETHIRI, PHERETRI, JUPITER-(THAT)-HATH-LED-ON-MY-CITY. "O God, when thou wentest forth before thy people, when thou marchedst out of the field of Edom, the earth trembled, and the heavens dropped."†

STATOR. This epithet, if referred to the Hebrew, may be derived from the obsolete טוּט, TUT, TO COLLECT, TO GATHER TOGETHER; אֲשֶׁר־טָט, ASHER-TAT, שֶׁטָּט, SHĔTAT, STAT, JUPITER-STAT, JUPITER-THE-RALLIER. "Ut Hostus cecidit, confestim Romana inclinatur acies; fusaque est ad veterem portam Palatii."‡

* Rom. xv.

† Psal. lxviii. 7. Jud. v. 4.

‡ Liv. i. 12.

TEMPLUM. תְּ־מְפְלוֹן, TĔMIPHLON, תְּמְפְלוֹן, TĔMPĔLON, TEMPLON, A-SEPARATED-PLACE, A-CONSECRATED-PLACE. The temples dedicated by Romulus to Jupiter, as the LEADER and RALLIER of the Romans, should seem to have been altars of the nature of those consecrated to the Almighty by Jacob and Moses. "And Jacob built an altar and called the place EL-BETH-EL; because there God appeared unto him." "And Moses built an altar, and called the name of it JEHOVAH-MY-BANNER."

SPOLIA OPIMA. Abraham, returning from the slaughter of the kings, gives a tithe of the spoil to Melchizedek, as the priest of the most high God, in token that he owns his victory to be from the Almighty; so the children of Judah offer to the Lord of the spoil which they have taken of the Ethiopians; and so, the Dictator Camillus * devotes to Apollo a tenth part of the spoils of the Veientes. Now the words SPOLIA OPIMA appear to contain the Hebrew following: אֲשֶׁר פֹּלֵא יָהּ עוֹף־אֵימָה, ASHER-POLE-IA-OPH-EMA, SE-POL-IA-OP-IMA, SPOLIAOPIMA, WHAT-JEHOVAH-THE-BRANDISHER-OF-TERROR-SEPARATES (or

* Liv. v. 21.

CONSECRATES). "And the terror of God (terror spread by God), was upon the cities that were round about them, and they did not pursue after the sons of Jacob."

QUIRINUS. קִיר־עַיִן, KIR-AYIN, קִירְעַיִן, KIREN, CITY-EYE, EYE-OF-THE-CITY. The epithet may be compared with the OCULUS MUNDI, or SUN, of the Romans.

NUMA POMPILIUS. Numa seems to be the Hebrew נְאֻם, with the emphatic ה. NEÜMA, NEUMA, NUMA, AN ORACLE; and Pompilius, פּוֹ־מְפִלְּהִי, PO-MEPILLEH-I, POMPILLI, HERE-(WAS)-MY-CONSECRATION, HERE-WAS-I-MADE-A-KING. POMPILI THE ORACULAR.

SACERDOS. סָגַר־עֵד, SACER-ED, SACERD, LOCKER-UP-(OR KEEPER)-OF-THE-TESTIMONY. In thirty-first Exodus,* the testimony denotes the commandments of God, written on two tables of stone.

DIALIS. דַּי־אֵל־אִישׁ, THE-ALMIGHTY'S-MAN; MAN-OF-JUPITER, called the (ALL)-SUFFICIENT-GOD.

FLAMEN. פָּלָא־אָמֵן, PALA-AMEN, פְּלָאמֵן, PELAMEN, PHLAMEN, CONSECRATED-IN-

* Verse 18.

PERPETUITY. It answers exactly to the SACERDOS ASSIDUUS of Livy.*

TARQUINIUS PRISCUS. LUCUMO. If the appellation PRISCUS be deriveable from the Hebrew,† and the names TARQUINIUS PRISCUS signify in reality TARQUINIAN SEPARATIST, SECEDER FROM TARQUINII, then LOCUMO, לא־קום־הוא, LOCOMO, לא־קומה, NOT-TO-RISE-ONE, NON-RISER, may be Hebrew also, an appellative given to the first Tarquin and other Etruscans by the Romans. "Anco regnante, LUCUMO,‡ vir impiger ac divitiis potens, Romam commigravit, cupidine maxime ac spe magni honoris, cujus adipiscendi Tarquiniis, nam ibi quoque peregrina stirpa oriundus erat, facultas non fuerat." "Lucumo," says Niebuhr,§ "is nowhere found in the Etruscan inscriptions, and the old philologians knew that it was no name."

ITALIA. This name, referred to the Hebrew (הִתַּלִּי־יה, HITTALLI-IA, HITTAL-IA, ITALIA), will mean MAYEST-THOU-BE-EXALTED-BY-JEHOVAH. The greatest uncertainty appears to exist respecting the locality and

* Lib. i. c. 20.

† Page 106.

‡ Liv. i. 34.

§ Lect. on Rom. Hist.

extent of the most ancient Italy. Regarded as an appellation originally confined to Rome and its territory, it would explain many of the prophecies by which the utter destruction of the mystical Edom is foretold; and a direct reference to it would then be found in the name given by the Romans to their city.

* * * *

The evidence of PROPHECY has next to be adduced in support of the TRADITION OF THE RABBINS, and in proof of the IDUMEAN ORIGIN of the ROMAN PEOPLE. Concerning the monster depicted in the thirteenth chapter of the Revelation of Saint John, Bishop Newton writes thus. "No doubt is to be made that this beast is designed to represent the Roman Empire; for, thus far, both ancients and moderns, papists and protestants, are agreed: the only controversy is, whether it be Rome Pagan or Christian, Imperial or Papal." Little less than the like agreement exists (as the Bishop also remarks), with regard to the dominion intended by the Fourth Beast of the prophecy of Daniel: "This fourth kingdom can be none other than the Roman Empire; and Calmet himself acknowledges that it is usually explained of the

Roman Empire." The prophecy of Saint John is, therefore, supplementary to that of Daniel, and from it we obtain much of the description of THE FOURTH KINGDOM UPON EARTH intentionally omitted by the Hebrew prophet; kept back, and reserved to be revealed in the fulness of time. The FOURTH BEAST, Daniel tells us, was "dreadful and terrible, and strong exceedingly; it had great iron teeth, and it had ten horns." Here the prophet stops. In other particulars, not noticed, this Beast was "diverse from all the Beasts that were before it." And for these diversities, and to complete the description of the Fourth Beast of Daniel, we must have recourse to the Revelation of Saint John. From his prophecy we learn that this Beast had "seven heads, and ten horns, and upon his horns ten crowns; that he was like unto a leopard; that his feet were as the feet of a bear, and his mouth as the mouth of a lion; that (like Esau) he was scarlet-coloured; and that upon his seven heads (representing seven hills) was seated a woman (or city), being that GREAT CITY which (when the vision was seen by the Apostle) reigned over all the kings (or kingdoms) of the earth." Of this Beast it is further written that "there was given unto him a mouth speaking great things and blasphemies;" also, "that it was given unto him to make war with the saints, and to overcome them;" and, also, "that power was given him over all kindreds, and tongues, and nations;" in the words of Daniel, "he was to devour the whole earth, and tread it down, and break it in pieces." The ten-horned Beast of Daniel being, then, identical with the ten-horned and seven-headed Beast of the Apocalypse, and each of them representing the Roman Empire in some stage of its existence, and during its progress to perdition, the prophecy further declares that the Beast has a numbered name, a name which (using its component letters as numerals) may be measured, or exhibited, by letters, amounting in the sum to six hundred and sixty-six. "Here is wisdom. Let him that hath understanding count the number (of the name) of the Beast: for it is the number (of the name) of a man; and his number (the number of his name) is SIX HUNDRED THREESCORE AND SIX." *"It is not, therefore,* a vain and ridiculous attempt to search into this mystery; but, on the contrary, it is recommended to us upon the authority of an apostle: the

* Bishop Newton.

number only is specified; and from the number we must, as well as we can, collect the name." But the prophecy does not declare in what language this name is to be counted; whether in the Greek of Saint John, the Hebrew of Daniel, or the mother-tongue of the Beast himself; and hence, perhaps, we may collect that it will be found in all of them, and (for this should seem essential to the certainty of the interpretation), in no other language of the earth. From the Greek, the late Dr. Adam Clarke has produced the words 'Η ΛΑΤΙΝΗ ΒΑΣΙΛΕΙΑ, one, we may well believe, of the names intended by the prophecy. Let us now see how much further the method of interpretation suggested by this commentator may be carried by means of the Hebrew of Daniel, being also the mother-tongue of Esau, the father of the Edomites. And the Hebrew, thus applied, discloses to us the following names, or descriptions, of the APOCALYPTIC BEAST; all comprising the number 666.

ממשל הרומה:

THE ROMAN EMPIRE.

מלכות האדמי והלטני:
מלכות אדמי ולטיני:

THE KINGDOM OF THE EDOMITE, OR LATIN.

ממשל האדומים והלטנים:
ממשל אדומים ולטינים:
ממשל אדומיים ולטנים:

THE EMPIRE OF THE EDOMITES, OR LATINS.

הממלכות לאדמים:

THE KINGDOM OF THE EDOMITES.

מלכות אדום ואדמי בנו:

THE KINGDOM OF EDOM, AND OF THE EDOMITE, HIS SON.

ממלכת אדמי ואדום אביהו:

THE KINGDOM OF THE EDOMITE, AND OF HIS FATHER, EDOM.

הממלכה של אדום הוא היה אבי האדמים:

THE KINGDOM OF EDOM: HE WAS THE FATHER OF THE EDOMITES.

והממלכה לעשו הוא אבי אדמים:

THE KINGDOM OF ESAU: HE WAS THE FATHER OF THE EDOMITES.

ממלכה לעשו ואדום אבי אדמי:

THE KINGDOM OF ESAU, ALIAS EDOM, THE FATHER OF THE EDOMITE.

* * * *

And in Italy, and on Rome, say the Rabbins, will the prophecies of the prophets against Esau, Edom, and the cities of Edom, be fulfilled. "The sword of the Lord is filled with blood: for the Lord hath a sacrifice in Bozrah, and a great slaughter in the land of Idumea. And the streams thereof shall be turned into pitch, and the dust thereof into brimstone, and the land thereof shall become burning pitch: it shall not be quenched night nor day; the smoke thereof shall go up for ever and ever: from generation to generation it shall lie waste; none shall pass through it for ever and ever." "Who is this that cometh from Edom, with dyed garments from Bozrah? this that is glorious in his apparel, travelling in the greatness of his strength? I that speak in righteousness, mighty to save. I have trodden the wine-press alone; and of the people there was none with me: for I will tread them in mine anger, and trample them in my fury; and their blood shall be sprinkled upon my garments, and I will stain all my raiment." "Whereas Edom saith, We are impoverished, but we will return and build the desolate places; thus saith the Lord of Hosts: They shall build; but I will throw down: and they shall call them THE BORDER OF WICKEDNESS, and, The people against whom the Lord hath indignation for ever." "And THE BEAST opened his mouth in BLASPHEMY AGAINST GOD; to blaspheme His name, and

His tabernacle, and Them that dwell in heaven." "And the great winepress of the wrath of God was trodden without the city, and blood came out of the winepress, even unto the horse-bridles, by the space of a thousand and six hundred furlongs." "And there was a great earthquake, such as was not since men were upon the earth so mighty an earthquake, and so great; and the GREAT CITY was divided into three parts; and the cities of the Gentiles fell; and BABYLON THE GREAT came in remembrance before God, to give unto her the cup of the wine of the fierceness of his wrath." "Her plagues shall come in one day, death, and mourning, and famine; and she shall be utterly burned with fire." "And the kings of the earth shall lament for her, when they shall see the smoke of her burning, saying, What city was like unto this great city." "With violence shall that great city Babylon be thrown down, and shall be found no more at all." "And the house of Jacob shall be a fire, and the house of Joseph a flame, and the house of Esau for stubble." "And saviours shall come up on Mount Zion to judge the house of Esau; and the KINGDOM SHALL BE THE LORD'S."*

* Rev. xix. 1, 2, 6.

APPENDIX.

THE INTERPRETATION ATTEMPTED OF THE PHŒNICIAN VERSES FOUND IN THE PŒNULUS OF PLAUTUS.

[WITH CORRECTIONS AND ADDITIONS.]

APPENDIX.

The fifth act of the Pœnulus opens with the appearance of The Carthaginian in the public streets, in search of his stolen daughters; and its first scene consists of a soliloquy delivered by The Bilinguis, partly in the languages of his own countrymen, and partly in the Latin of his Roman audience. Of the sixteen verses which constitute the Punic portion of this soliloquy, I treat the first ten as belonging to the Phœnician, or Canaanitish, tongue: the remaining six, together with the shorter, non-Latin, speeches of Hanno and the Nurse, found in the two succeeding scenes of the same act, I refer to the Libyc dialect of the soliloquist.

Amongst the host of scholars who have laboured at the elucidation of these verses, two only, Bochart and Gesenius, have produced anything approaching to an interpretation of them; and of their expositions it may here be sufficient to observe, that they are, for the most part, contradictory and subversive of each other; exhibiting little more than the discordant results of conjectural criticism, employed in the emendation of a text which (in the judgment of the critics), the mistakes of the copyists have rendered all but incurably defective, and irretrievably depraved. BOCHART, referring to the common text, as printed in his Phaleg, terms it, "Decem versus prout corrupte scribuntur in Plauti editionibus:" "Certum est," writes GESENIUS, "omniumque criticorum consensu approbatum, Plautinarum fabularum exempla, nedum Punicam Pœnuli orationem, librariorum inscitia et incuria, nævos contraxisse, sine antiquiorum meliorumque librorum auxilio, vix sanabiles;" and also, speaking of these verses, "Nonnulli versus ita comparati sunt, ut vulgatæ scripturæ neque medela, neque explicatio probabilis, inventa sit." To refer to the SECOND VERSE, "difficillimus omnium," as Gesenius calls it: of the forty-two letters of which it is composed, no less than twenty-one have been treated as spurious by the one or the other of these learned writers. By Bochart this line is read, CHI MELACHAI NITTHEMU MATSLIA MIDDABAREHEM ISKI: and by Gesenius, CHYM LACCHU YTH TUMMY

'STHYAL MYTTHIBARIIM ISCHI: the one translates it, "Ut consilia mea compleantur, prosperum sit ex ductu eorum negotium meum;" the other, "Ut, ubi abstulerunt prosperitatem meam, impleatur, jussu eorum, desiderium meum,"

In attempting the interpretation of the TEN VERSES, I venture to controvert the received opinion of the learned; and to contend, that the substantial integrity of this portion of the existing copies of the Pœnulus has been unnecessarily, and unjustly, impugned by the critics.

The printed copies of the comedy are derived, we are told, from three manuscripts; to be found, one at Rome, another at Heidelberg, and the third at Leipsic. The text of the EDITIO PRINCEPS, printed at Venice in the year 1472, will be used for the purposes of the present investigation: it is said by Gesenius to approach most nearly to that of the LEIPSIC MS. According to this edition, the TEN VERSES contain three hundred and seventy-eight letters; and of these the mistakes imputable to the copyists affect, I would say, at the utmost, but eighteen; and in one instance only do the corrections they render necessary call for the rejection or change of more than a single letter of the word.

Moreover, the emendations proposed have little of a conjectural character, but appear to be clearly pointed to by the context: two of them are to be met with in the Roman MS., and another in the Plautus of Robert Stephens, dating in the year 1530. For instance, if, in the SECOND VERSE, we discard, with the Roman MS., the third CH, and change a succeeding T into an L, we regain, I imagine, the true reading of the line: CHYMLACHUN YTH MUMYSLY ALMYCTHY BARIIIM ISCHI.

The corrections which the text of the EDITIO PRINCEPS appears to require will stand as follows, the FIRST and FIFTH VERSES being treated as absolutely intact.

Second Verse.

Reject CH, reading CHYMLACHUN (Roman MS.), for CHYMLACHCHUN; and change T into L, reading MUMYSLY for MUMYSTY.

Third Verse.

Insert R, reading LIPHORCAN for LIPHOCAN.

Fourth Verse.

Reject R, reading BYN for BYRN.

Sixth Verse.

Change E into A, reading YSSIDA for YSSIDE; insert Y, reading YTHYFEL for THYFEL; and change U into E, reading LIPHEL for LIPHUL.

Seventh Verse.

Reject Y, reading DIBURTHI (Robert Stephens), for DIBURTHYI.

Eighth Verse.

Change H into Y, reading ELYCOTYS for ELYCOTHS.

Ninth Verse.

Change I into E, reading BYNNIED for BYNNIID; change G into C, reading HILIC for HILIG; change U into Y, and N into M, reading UBYLIM for UBULIN (Roman MS. UBULIM); and insert E, reading ITTEHYM for ITTHYM.

Tenth Verse.

Reject Y, reading ALTHERA for ALYTHERA; reject U, reading YNNYNNYS for YNNYNNUYS; insert A, reading AMON for MON; and change H into I, reading COTI for COTH.

The amended text may be thus translated.

First Verse.

NOW, ON THE GODS AND THE GODDESSES OF THIS PLACE DO I CALL,

Second Verse.

TO PURGE AWAY MY STAINS, THAT SO I MAY BECOME A SPOTLESS MAN; TO

Third Verse.

QUICKLY BRING TO ME MY DAUGHTERS, MY DAUGHTERS, THE DELIGHT OF MY OLD AGE.

Fourth Verse.

SHOULD ONE OFFER THE GODS THAT GIVE INCREASE OF THE INCREASE THAT CAN'T BE ONE'S OWN?

Fifth Verse.

IF DEATH DIDN'T STAND IN MY WAY, I SHOULD LODGE AT ANTIDAMAS' HOUSE.

Sixth Verse.

OF THE TROOP THAT PERAMBULATE DARKNESS IS HE, THE HOSTS THAT IN DARKNESS HAVE HOMES:

Seventh Verse.

AND (AIN'T I SO TOLD?) AGORASTOCLES IS THE SON THAT LAMENTS HIM.

Eighth Verse.

I BRING WITH ME, SEE! 'TIS HIS GIFT, A GRAVING, A CUT-IN-TWAIN GOD;

Ninth Verse.

A WITNESS 'TWIXT ME AND THE HOUSE-GODS, IF HEAVEN HAS LED ME TOWARDS THEM.

Tenth Verse.

HERE I STAND 'MIDST THE CROWDS THAT PASS BY: A LOT HAVE THEY 'MONGST THEM WHO FOREIGNERS CANNOT ABIDE.

I proceed to exhibit the original and corrected text of the Editio Princeps in three forms. First, the letters of each verse will be set out in an unbroken series, distinguishing, by asterisks placed over them, such as are to be withdrawn from the line, and including between brackets the letters to be introduced into it. Next, the corrected contents of the verse will be drawn from it, and distributed into distinct words. Lastly, the amended text will be transcribed in Hebrew letters, adding thereto the points in the few cases where the pronunciation differs from the received punctuation of the Hebrew. To the production of this text some preliminary observations will be necessary.

And, first. Although the contents of the TEN VERSES satisfactorily establish the original identity of the Carthaginian and Hebrew tongues, they yet present us with some forms the use of which the sacred writers have declined. We have, then, the word אתי, existing as a pronoun of the first person singular. The full form occurs in the first, second, and eighth verses; whilst as a suffix, תי, it is found in the seventh. The undoubted derivation of the second person singular of the past tense of the Hebrew verb from the root, and a pronoun taking the forms אֲתָה and אַתָּה, might lead us to conclude that the first person singular of the same tense must be a compound of the root and a pronoun, having the forms אֲתִי, אַתִּי; and the same pronoun may also enter into the composition of the Hebrew objective אותי. Since both אני and אתי appear to have been in use amongst the Carthaginians, both are perhaps contractions of a longer word, אַנְתִּי. Next, we find the verb with a prefixed שׁ; a form seemingly emphatic, and analogous to the shaphel of the Syriac. It occurs in the first, and (as I think) in the sixth verse also: in this last, however, the letters are susceptible of more than one interpretation. Then, we have not only ל and של, but also שׁ used as signs of the genitive; and in the sixth verse, where two genitives come together, the first has the prefix שׁ, and the other ל. The places of two nouns in the state of definite construction are sometimes transposed, and the noun in the genitive put first; but this, as, also, the use of the construct for the absolute form of the noun, may be regarded as poetical licences. The feminine plural ends in ות; and the punctuation of הוּא, as a pronoun masculine of the third person, is הִוא. Lastly, a fondness for the vowel E appears; whether this be a characteristic of the Phœnician generally, or a peculiarity confined to the language as spoken by the Carthaginians. Thus, we have זֵאת for זאת; אֵפֵל for אפל; שֵׁרֵת for שָׁרַת: (perhaps) also, מֵחוֹה for מָחוֹה; and בֵּנוֹת for בָּנוֹת.

The form into which Plautus has thrown the words of the original will also require attention. Throughout these verses an initial י is treated by the poet as a vowel, taking (so to speak) the sound of the point attached to it; and, as with the Greeks, the letter שׁ is always represented by the unaspirated S. For יֵשׁ, therefore, we have YS; for יִשֵׁרֵת, ISYRYTH; IMLACH for יִמְלַח; ETHU for יֵתוּ; and IS for אִישׁ. In most cases Y represents the TSERE of the Hebrews, and is considered as equivalent to I. I:

as, YTH for אֵת; CHYMLACH for כִּימַלְּח; and LYM for לִיאִם. The first verse comprises eighteen syllables, reduced, by the elision of three vowels, to fifteen, the average length of the Latin hexameter; and a determination that all the verses shall have the same length seems to be clearly evinced. To effect this, in the second verse a syllable is added to the word בָּרִים, which is here trisyllábic. In two instances a final י takes the form I. I; as BYNUTHII for בנותי, and OTHII for אותי. In the last case, this form appears to add a syllable to the word.

With these introductory remarks, I offer my reading of the TEN VERSES to the judgment of the learned.

First Verse.

N. Y. T. H. A. L. O. N. I. M. V. A. L. O. N. U. T. H. S. I. C. O. R. A. T. H. I. S. I. M. A. C. O. M. S. Y. T. H.

NYTH ALONIM VALONUTH SICORATHI SIMACOM SYTH.

נא את אלונים ואלונות שְׁקוֹרֵא אֲתִי שמקום זֵאת

Second Verse.

C. H. Y. M. L. A. C. H. C̈. Ḧ. U. N. Y. T. H. M.

U. M. Y. S. T. [L.] Y. A. L. M. Y. C. T. H. I. B. A. R. I. I. I, M. I. S. C. H. I.

CHYMLACHUN YTH MUMYSLY ALMYC-THI BARIIIM ISCHI.

כי ימלחון את מומים יש לי על מחה אֱתִי בריים איש כי

Third Verse.

L. I. P. H. O. [R.] C. A. N. E. T. H. Y. T. H. B. Y. N. U. T. H. I. I. A. D. A. E. D. I. N. B. Y. N. U. T. H. I. I.

LIPHORCAN ETHYTH BYNUTHII AD' AËDIN BYNUTHII.

לי פורחן יתו את בֱנוּתי עדי העדן בֱנוּתי

Fourth Verse.

B. Y. R. N. A. R. O. B. S. Y. L. L. O. H. O. M. A. L. O. N. I. N. U. B. Y. M. I. S. Y. R. T. H. O. H. O.

'BYN AROB SYLLOHO 'MALONI NUBYM ISYRTHOHO.

מבין הרוב של לא הוּא אם אלוני נובים יְשֻרתו הוּא

Fifth Verse.

B. Y. T. H. L. Y. M. M. O. T. H. Y. N. N. O. C. T. O. T. H. I. I. V. E. L. E. C. A. N. T. I. D. A. S. M. A. C. H. O. N.

BYTHLYM MOTHYN NOCTOTHII VELEC ANTIDAS MACHON.

בית לי אם מות אין נחת אותי בהלך אנטידמס מכון

Sixth Verse.

Y. S. S. I. D. Ė. [A.] L. E. B. R. I. M. [Y.] T. H. Y. F. E. L. Y. T. H. C. H. Y. L. Y. S. C. H. O. N. T. H. E. M. L. I. P. H. U̇. [E.] L.

YSSIDA LEBRIM YTHYFEL YTHCHYLY SCHONTHEM LIPHEL.

יש שעדה לְעֲברים את אֶפל את חלי שקנתים לאפל

Seventh Verse.

U. T. H. B. Y. N. I. M. Y. S. D. I. B. U. R. T. H. Ẏ. I. N. N. O. C. U. T. H. N. U. A. G. O. R. A. S. T. O. C. L. E. S.

UTHBYN IMYS DIBURTHI 'NNOCUTHNU AGORASTOCLES.

ואת בן אם יש דברתי הנאקותינו אגורסטוקלס

Eighth Verse.

Y. T. H. E. M. A. N. E. T. H. I. H. Y. C. H. I. R. S. A. E. L. Y. C. O. T. Ḣ. [Y.] S. I. T. H. N. A. S. O.

YTHE MANETHI HY CHIRSA ELYCOTYS ITHNASO.

אֶתִי מאנה אֲתִי הא חִרְשָׁה אליקוט יש אתנה שהוֹא

Ninth Verse.

B. Y. N. N. I. İ. [E.] D. C. H. I. L. L. U. H. I. L. I. Ġ. [C.] U. B. U̇. [Y.] L. I. Ṅ. [M.] L. A. S. I. B. I. T. T. [E.] H. Y. M.

BYNNIED CHILLU HILIC UBYLIM LASIB' ITTEHYM.

בֵּינֵי עד כי אלו היליך ובין אלים לשיבה אתהם

Tenth Verse.

B. O. D. Y. A. L. Y̊. T. H. E. R. A. Y. N. N. Y. N. N. Ů. Y. S. L. Y. M. [A.] M. O. N. C. O. T. H̊. [I.] L. U. S. I. M.

BODY ALTHERA YNNYNNYS LYM AMON COTILUSIM.

בעדים על תרע הנני יש להם הטח קומי לוצים

OBSERVATIONS.

First Verse.—ALONIM. אלונים and אלהים appear to be different forms of the same word, and to be derived from אל: אֶל־הוּא, Mighty-one; אֱלֹה, אֱלֹן, אֱלוֹנִים, אֱלֹהִים. The terminations הּ and ןֹ are equivalents; so שְׁלֹמֹה, is written by the Septuagint translators Σαλωμων, or שְׁלֹמֹן, that is, שָׁלוֹם־הוּא. MACOM. So Abraham uses מקום for עיר (Gen. xviii. 24). It is singular that, with the story of Abdalonymus, as related by Quintus Curtius, before him, Bochart should insist on reading Elyon, in this verse, for

Alonim. For Abdalonym is עֶבֶד־אֱלֹנִים, Servus Deorum.

Second Verse.—CHYMLACHUN. מלח, which in Ezekiel signifies *To rub with salt*, as part of the customary purifications of the new-born child, is here used in the sense of *purging*, or *purifying*, in general. An allusion to infant purity may, perhaps, be intended. So Shakspeare, "Till the foul deeds done in my course of nature are burnt and purged away." We have here the paragogic or emphatic ן, following כי; and the Moveable Sheva is represented (as is commonly the case in the Septuagint), by the letter A. MUMYSLY. The reading may be מומי שלי; Hanno, perhaps, referring to some particular sin, punished by the gods with the loss of his daughters. ALMYCTHI. מחה has here the secondary signification observable in Numb. xxxiv. 11, *To reach to*, *To attain to*; and hence, as we say, *To be come*. BARIM. אִישׁ בָּרִים, the intensive plural of בור.

Third Verse.—LIPHORCAN, An adverb פֹּרְחָן, or פֹּרְחָם, formed, I imagine, from the participle of פרח, and signifying, literally, *Flyingly*.

Fourth Verse.—SYLLOHO. שֶׁל לֹא הוּא, for לֹא שֶׁלוֹ. "We have nothing," says Hanno, "but what has been given us by the gods; and to affect to give to them, when we can only do so out of their own gifts, is absurd. So David, "All things come of Thee; and of Thine own have we given Thee." (1 Chron. xxix. 14.) ISYRTHO. Piel of שרת, with the paragogic ו, the occurrence of which in the Hebrew as an addition to the verb has been doubted.

SIXTH VERSE.—LEBRIM. עֹבֵר, a verbal from עבר, and signifying, Passer-on, Pilgrim. It occurs in Gen. x. 21, where it has been mistaken for a proper-name: "Shem," says Moses, "was the father of all the בְּנֵי עֵבֶר, all the sons of 'Passing-on,' 'Pilgrimage;' all who, after the flood, betook themselves to the Nomadic life. Hence Abraham had the appellation העברי, THE HEBREW, THE PILGRIM, whether adopted by himself or bestowed on him by the Almighty; because, in obedience to the command of God, he entered on and endured a pilgrimage which was to end only with his life. SCHONTHEM. The text may be read, את חל יש קונתים.

SEVENTH VERSE.—'NNOCUTHNU. A verbal, as it seems, from נאק, and equivalent to נְאָקָה. The suffix may be the singular, ־ֶנּוּ; but it seems rather to be the plural ־ֵנוּ; Hanno here using that jocular form of speaking which puts the plural for the singular; 'Our-sorrowing-son,' or, in the idiom of the Hebrew, 'The-son-of-our-sorrows.' That such method of expression is not inconsistent with the character, appears from the subsequent verses, in which the Carthaginian is made to say, speaking of his deceased friend Antidamas, 'Eum fecisse aiunt sibi quod faciendum fuit.'

Eighth Verse.—CHIRSA. I take this to be חֶרֶשׂ with the emphatic ה postfixed. Other words derived to the Greeks from the Phœnicians exhibit the same formation: as אַלְפָּה for הָאָלֶף; נַבְלָה for הַנֶּבֶל. May not even אֱלוֹהַּ be an example of the same form: אלדדה for האלדוא, The-Almighty-one. Chirsa Elycot: Tessara Dimidiata: Deus Hospitalis.

Ninth Verse.—CHILLU. The force of כי appears to be lost, as in the כי אם of the Hebrew. ITTEHYM. The punctuation of the Hebrew, and the consideration that without the inserted E the line would have but fourteen syllables, appear to warrant the addition of this letter, or the Moveable Sheva.

Tenth Verse.—BODYM ALTHERA. 'The-goers-before-the-door,' the 'Passengers-in-the-streets.'

YNNYNNYS. The reading may be YNNYNU YSYLYM, הננו יש לדם, as in the Editio Princeps; Hanno here including himself and his audience. If this reading be adopted, the A, inserted to complete the number of syllables, must be withdrawn; and we must read 'MON for AMON.

The similarity of structure observable in the Carthaginian of Hanno and the Hebrew of Moses and the Prophets, sufficiently identifies both languages with the Phœnician; and the identity of the Phœnician and the Hebrew tongues established, it follows, that the Israelites received their language from the descendants of Canaan, the son of Ham; and that the Hebrew of the Bible is no other than the Canaanitish, or Phœnician, tongue, expressed in the Chaldaic character, the character brought (we may well believe) by Abraham himself from Ur of the Chaldees. But the books of Moses offer us evidence, hardly to be resisted, that the language of his writings was, also, the language of the Antediluvian World; and hence it follows, further, that in the grand confusion of languages at Babel the primitive tongue was continued to mankind in the line of Canaan; and so, by a circuitous providence, the language spoken by the Second Adam was (in the main) the language of THE FIRST. The Scriptures afford no countenance to the philology which aims at establishing the original identity of all languages, and reproducing the common mother of them all, the tongue spoken by Noah when he issued from the ark. They teach us that human speech is not derived from one, but many mothers; mothers created (with one exceptión) in the same hour; standing towards each other in the relationship of sisters; and holding, therefore, amongst themselves, equal and independent rank. The Syriac, Chaldee, and Arabic, may be derivatives from the Phœnician, and may owe their existence to the great outspread of Canaan's sons, (Gen. x. 18); or they may be primitive and distinct tongues, designed by their Creator to evince how near in structure one language may approach another, and yet the end of their creation be obtained, and the speakers of them be unintelligible to each other. (Isa. xxvi. 11; Jer. v. 15.)

The TEN VERSES afford an argument, conclusive against the system of those Hebraists who deny the authenticity of the pronunciation preserved and perpetuated by the Masoretic punctuation of the Hebrew Scriptures, and greatly in favour of the origin and antiquity attributed to 'the points' by the tradition of the Jews. 'The points,' say the Jews, 'were from Moses; but were first added to the letters by Ezra:' (in other words) The pronunciation of the Hebrew indicated by the Masoretic punctuation is as old as Moses, and was, indeed, 'from the beginning;' but 'the points' by which it has been derived to us were excogitated, and first added to the letters, by this great scribe. How slight the difference between the pronunciation of the Phœnician, as spoken at Carthage in the days of Plautus, and that delivered to us by the Punctuists as the pronunciation of the Hebrew in the times of Dido and the Israelitish kings!

CORRIGENDA.

Page 12, line 21—*for* comminuat, *read* comminuet.

Page 41, line 23—*for* Lycophron of Cassandra, *read* Cassandra of Lycophron.

Page 62, line 15—*for* שְׁלָי־אֵל, *read* שְׁלָת־יְ־אֵל.

Page 75, line 14—*for* other words, *read* other verbs of this class.

Page 78, lines 11 and 12—*for* I-MUST-BE, *read* I MUST BE; *and for* HE-MUST-BE, *read* HE MUST BE.

Page 87, line 13—*for* תְּרוֹיָהּ, *read* תְּרֹעְיָהּ.

Page 88, line 7—*for* punctum-glutationis, *read* punctum-glutinationis.

CPSIA information can be obtained
at www.ICGtesting.com
Printed in the USA
BVHW03s1438100518
515765BV00007B/179/P